DECISION-MAKING FOR DEFENSE

Decision-Making for Defense

By Charles J. Hitch

UNIVERSITY OF CALIFORNIA PRESS
BERKELEY AND LOS ANGELES 1965

University of California Press
Berkeley and Los Angeles, California

Cambridge University Press
London, England

H. ROWAN GAITHER LECTURES IN SYSTEMS SCIENCE

The Gaither Memorial Lectures in Systems Science were set up by gift of System Development Corporation—formerly a division of the RAND Corporation, which Mr. Gaither helped to organize. The Gaither Lectures are to be given each year for five years and are arranged by the Graduate School of Business Administration and the Center for Research in Management Science of the University of California, Berkeley.

CHARLES J. HITCH was the first lecturer in this series.

Contents

I | 1789-1960

I AM DEEPLY HONORED to be invited to deliver the first series of Gaither Memorial Lectures. Rowan Gaither was a man of many and diverse interests, but I think that nothing interested him more than the problem of improving the process of reaching defense decisions. He would be pleased, I am sure, by the subject I have selected, if not by the substance. His own contributions to defense decision-making were significant and durable.

He served as an official of one of the earliest fruitful partnerships of government, science, and industry—the wartime Radiation Laboratory of the Massachusetts Institute of Technology—which has been a model for so many later similar enterprises.

He was a founder and the first Chairman of the Board of the RAND Corporation, where many of the techniques that I will be discussing this week were first developed and applied. RAND was one of Gaither's consuming interests, and he served as Chairman of its Board until his death four years ago.

He was head of the famous "Gaither Committee," and his influential, although secret, report on the Nation's defenses in 1957 surveyed both the substance of defense decisions and the methods of defense decision-making.

To give you an idea of the spirit in which Rowan Gaither approached the problem of defense decision-making, I can do no better than quote from one of his last public statements, made to the Board of RAND Corporation on the occasion of that organization's tenth anniversary in late 1958:

The war in which we will be engaged for years to come places burdens unprecedented in their complexity and consequence upon our government. Ways must be found to increase the competence of government personnel at all levels. Administratively our government must make improvements in the process of decision-making. I am sure I do not have to prove to this Board that political as well as physical survival may well turn on the speed and efficiency with which technology is converted into weapons and weapon systems. Nor need I argue that the war in which we are engaged is no longer, and perhaps not even predominantly, one of materiel and men; it is a war in which the economic and political factors have assumed crucial importance, in fact, may become the decisive factors. All this means is that government is not self-sufficient—if indeed it ever was—and that if it is to meet the threat it will be increasingly dependent upon our intellectual, our scientific and our economic resources. Not only must these resources be readily available, but they must be competent, they must be responsible. We must find the organizational instrumentalities for bringing our resources to bear on the task of survival by assuring their responsible availability to government.[1]

In a most significant way, this is exactly what we have been trying to do in the Defense Department during the past four years, that is, to find the best "organizational instrumentalities for bringing our resources to bear on the task of survival." In these four lectures, I will review that search:

In this first lecture, I will trace the evolution of the "defense problem" over the course of our nation's history under the Constitution. I believe this will help you understand the nature of the decision-making process in the 1960's and why certain improvements in that process were needed in January 1961.

In the second lecture, I will describe the purpose and function of the "programming" system which we installed in 1961 and how it fits into the over-all management of the defense establishment.

In the third lecture I will describe our efforts to apply the techniques

---

[1] For notes, see page 79.

of operations research or systems analysis to the problem of defense decision-making particularly with regard to the choice of weapon systems and the allocation of resources among alternative forces and programs.

In the final lecture, I will attempt, as best I can, to evaluate these innovations, to discuss the unresolved problems in their application and to assess their place in the future.

Although I will be focusing my attention in these lectures on the decision-making process within the Defense Department itself, I am sure you understand that all major defense decisions must be made within the much broader context of our total national security policy. As Rowan Gaither pointed out, ". . . the war in which we are engaged is no longer, and perhaps not even predominantly, one of materiel and men; it is a war in which the economic and political factors have assumed crucial importance, in fact, may become the decisive factors." Indeed, defense decisions cannot be divorced, in peace or in war, from political, economic, and technological considerations. At the highest level of government, all four aspects of national security policy must be taken into account simultaneously, and the defense decision-making process must be so designed as to contribute to that endeavor.

When the Founding Fathers assembled in Philadelphia to draft the Constitution of the United States, the Nation was small and weak. The population of the thirteen colonies numbered about three and one-half million.[2] Although we had natural resources in great abundance, the means for exploiting them were very limited. Manufacture was in its infancy and means of communication most primitive. Under these conditions, it was not surprising that our national security objectives were very modest, namely, to avoid foreign entanglements, to defend the land frontiers against the Indians and our neighbors in Canada and Florida, and to maintain internal security. Of the three, defense against the Indians appeared to many to be the most important.[3]

For this purpose, a small permanent military establishment was considered quite sufficient and principal reliance to meet emergencies was placed on the states' militia, which, incidentally, was to be supported by the states without cost to the Federal Government.[4] To manage this small establishment, a War Department was created, headed by a Secretary who was also a member of the President's Cabinet. In the very

first year, our military establishment consisted only of ground forces—
an Army of 46 officers and 672 men.[5]

A Navy was considered far too expensive for so young a nation, heavily
burdened as it was with debts accumulated during the War for Independence. Not until 1793 was consideration given to the construction of a
Navy. Under the prodding of the depredations inflicted on American
shipping by the Barbary pirates in the Mediterranean as well as by
French Republican privateers operating in our own home waters, President George Washington in his fifth State of the Union Message to the
Congress on December 3, 1793, warned: "I cannot recommend to your
notice measures for the fullfilment [sic] of our duties to the rest of the
world without again pressing upon you the necessity of placing ourselves in a condition of compleat defence, and of exacting from them
the fullfilment of their duties toward us . . . There is a rank due to the
United States among Nations, which will be withheld, if not absolutely
lost, by the reputation of weakness. If we desire to avoid insult, we must
be able to repel it; if we desire to secure peace . . . it must be known,
that we are at all times ready for War."[6]

On March 27, 1794, the Congress authorized the building of six large
frigates to form the backbone of a new, seagoing United States Navy.
This task was undertaken by the War Department. Six private yards,
so selected as to spread the work among the states as equitably as possible
and with greatest political advantage, were leased.[7] However, the construction moved along very slowly, since, among other reasons, supplies
had to be purchased in Europe, which was then in the midst of a war
between France and England. It was not until the end of 1795 that the
six keels were finally laid, nearly seventeen months after the construction had been authorized. Shortly thereafter, partly as a result of mismanagement, delays, and cost overruns, the program was cut back to
three frigates.

Even then the War Department encounted great difficulty in getting
the work completed. Growing dissatisfaction with the performance of
the War Department as a shipbuilder gave rise to clamor for the establishment of a separate Department of the Navy. Among the arguments
advanced by the proponents were the following:

The Secretary of War already had more than one man could do and
therefore could not properly attend to the increasing Naval business.

The Congress had appropriated so much money for Naval affairs that an expert was needed to manage them economically.

A Naval Department was necessary to impress Europe—particularly France.

The opponents of the new department argued that:

If more help were needed, experts and additional clerks could be added to the Department of War.

The establishment of a Navy Department would not impress Europe since it would be little more than a gesture.

The revenue of the United States was not sufficient to support so large a navy as to require a separate department for its administration.

I would not want to question the originality of C. Northcote Parkinson's great contribution to the theory of public administration, but I must record here that the House Committee considering the bill clearly noted that the establishment of a new department would not necessarily result in economy because every new governmental institution had a tendency to aggrandize itself. Thought was given to establishing a Commissioner of Marine in the Department of War, but in the end this solution was rejected as inadequate. The final argument advanced by the proponents was that if the new department proved to be useless, it could always be abolished![8] Clearly the proponents lacked the full benefit of Parkinson's wisdom.

And so, in the spring of 1798, the Department of the Navy was established; the cause of "unification" was lost for the next century and a half. Ten weeks after the Department of the Navy was established, the Congress created a Marine Corps, which the President was free to use either aboard ship or to garrison fortifications. The Marines were to take the oath and obey the regulations of both the Army and the Navy. Thus, by the close of the eighteenth century, the U.S. defense establishment consisted of two executive departments and a separate corps, and it was not until 1834 that an Act of Congress placed the Marine Corps completely under the control of the Secretary of the Navy.

With the continued growth of the Nation came the westward expansion and a great increase in overseas trade. The first created problems with the Indians who were being supported by the British. The second ran afoul of the continuing conflict between England and France. The resulting stresses on land and sea culminated in the War of 1812 and in a large increase, for that time, in the military establishment. With the end of that war the military establishment was cut back, but it was clear that the Navy was here to stay.[9]

Indeed, in 1823 the role of the Navy was further enhanced by the expansion of our national security objectives to include the defense of the western hemisphere. I refer, of course, to the doctrine enunciated by President Monroe in his seventh State of the Union Message. By this time the population of the United States exceeded ten million[10] and the Louisiana Territory had been acquired and partly settled. Manufacturing had increased dramatically, Army arsenals and Navy shipyards had been established, and the new nation had begun to feel its strength.

The westward expansion and the rounding out of the present United States continued throughout most of the nineteenth century. Toward the close of that century, America started to look outward. Under the prodding of Admiral Mahan and others, attention was directed to the United States Navy as a means of enhancing our position in the world. American technology had reached a point where it could produce most of the materials and components required for the construction of steel warships, and this technology was demonstrated in late 1889 when a squadron of four new steel ships began a cruise which took them to the principal ports of Europe. With the successful termination of the Spanish-American War and the resulting acquisition of territorial possessions in the Caribbean and the far Pacific, our national security objectives were further expanded, and the case for a modern two-ocean Navy was firmly established. The expansion of our national interests beyond the borders of the continental United States also placed greater responsibilities on the Army and, indeed, an expeditionary force was dispatched to the Philippines in 1899 to re-establish law and order.[11] Thus, by the close of the nineteenth century, the United States was well on its way to establishing itself as a world power.

This great expansion of national objectives, together with the growth in the size and power of the military establishment, would in itself have required some changes in the organization and procedures for the management of the defense effort. But during the nineteenth century military technology had also advanced dramatically. The time when armies could be mobilized by calling up the militia—each militiaman with his own rifle, ammunition, and personal equipment—had long since gone, even by the War of 1812. Although the instruments of war of the nineteenth century were primitive by today's standards, they were steadily becoming more complex and more numerous and of greater variety. Major development and production efforts were required to provide them and "logistics," in the broadest sense of the term, took on an increasing importance in the administration of the defense establishment.

As the Army grew in the early years of our history and its supply and administration became more complex, the organization of the War Department began to proliferate. It started with a so-called General Staff, consisting of an Adjutant General, a Quartermaster General, and a Commissary General of Ordnance, plus a separate Chief of Engineers; in 1818 a Judge Advocate General and a Surgeon General were added, and later, still more staff offices. These predecessors of the so-called technical and staff services of the Army became firmly established as statutory institutions in their own right and created major problems of coordination and command within the War Department itself. A similar trend toward a proliferation of specialties manifested itself in the Navy, and, in 1842, culminated with the establishment of the bureaus, creating the same kind of problems within that department.

It was not until 1903, following the great difficulties encountered in the management of the Spanish-American War, that a beginning was made in solving the problem within the War Department. Ever since 1821, when a Commanding General of the Army was appointed, the Army had been plagued by a system of dual control. Army regulations prescribed that "The military establishment is under orders of the Commanding General of the Army in that which pertains to its discipline and military control. The fiscal affairs of the Army are conducted by the Secretary of War, through the several staff departments."[12] This organizational doctrine gave rise to endless confusion, misunderstanding, and friction. The regulation was interpreted to mean that the Secretary of War had no control of the Army in the field while the Commanding General had no control of the resources required to support the Army.[13] The latter was the responsibility of the "General Staff" operating under the Secretary of War, and each of the staff departments of the War Department considered itself virtually autonomous, thus impeding a coordinated, not to speak of a unified, effort.

This situation so galled General Sherman, who succeeded Grant as Commanding General in May 1869, that he decided in September 1874 to remove his office to St. Louis where he could at least escape "the mortifications of being slighted by men in Washington who were using their temporary power for selfish ends."[14]

It fell to Secretary of War Root to solve this problem of dual control. His solution was straightforward. The Secretary of War should be the undisputed head of the Army under the President. There should be no military commander independent of the Secretary of War. The senior general at the War Department should be the responsible advisor and executive agent of the Secretary, serving not as a commander in his own right but as Chief of Staff to his civilian superior. In no other way, Root felt, would it be possible to maintain that supremacy of civilian over military authority which had been so basic to the concept of Government in the United States from the very beginning.[15] In February 1903, the Congress enacted his recommendations.[16] The Office of Chief of Staff, supported by a new General Staff corps, was created and the position of the Commanding General was abolished. The old "General Staff" departments were placed under the direction of the Chief of Staff, although it took another decade for the Chief of Staff to establish unquestioned authority over them.[17]

In 1915, a parallel development took place in the Navy with the creation of the Office of Chief of Naval Operations which was to have under its control war planning and fleet operations, corresponding to many of the functions of a general staff. Some twenty-five years earlier, the Secretary of the Navy had taken steps to break down the compartmentalization of the bureaus which, like those in the War Department, had considered themselves autonomous to the point of refusing to transfer stocks from one bureau to another.[18]

But the Spanish-American War had focused attention sharply on yet another problem, which is still a matter of some controversy today. I speak here of the problem of unification, of concerting the efforts of all elements of the national defense establishment—ground, sea, and air. We often forget how recently even nominal unification of the defense effort was achieved and how difficult this achievement was.

The advantages of combined operations of land and sea forces were clearly recognized by our first Commander in Chief during the War for Independence. General George Washington, although distinctly a "landlubber," had a very keen appreciation of the value of naval power in the kind of war we had to fight against the British, who held control of the sea off the Atlantic coast.[19] In writing to the Marquis de Lafayette in November 1781, General Washington pointed out, ". . . No land force can act decisively unless it is accompanied by a Maritime superiority. . . . for proof of this, we have only to recur to the instances of the ease and facility with which the British shifted their ground as advantages were to be obtained at either extremity of the Continent. . . ."[20]

But despite Washington's appreciation of sea power, the Colonies had difficulty enough in supporting even a modest army, let alone a navy which would be in any way a match for the British fleet. Thus, it was not until France entered the war on a large scale that Washington was given an opportunity to put his theory into practice. When a French fleet under the command of Count d'Estaing appeared off the Atlantic coast in the fall of 1779, he was quick to press for a combined operation against New York City. The French Admiral, however, preferred to fight the British fleet in the Caribbean. But Washington persevered, and finally, in the summer of 1781, with much cajoling and much flattering, he persuaded Count de Grasse— in command of a large French fleet then in American waters—to join him in a combined operation against the British at Yorktown. The French fleet was to "bottle up" the British on the seaward while he marched on Yorktown from the landward.

The operation proceeded well, but in late September Count de Grasse informed Washington that, in his opinion, he could do more good with his fleet in the waters around New York City than he could by merely standing by off Cape Henry as a "spectator." In great anguish Washington wrote to the Admiral:

Sir: I cannot conceal from your Excellency the painful anxiety under which I have labored since the receipt of the letter with which you honored me on the 23d inst . . . the enterprise against York under the protection of your Ships, is as certain as any military operation can be rendered by a decisive superiority of strength and means; that it is in fact reducible to calculation, and that the surrender of the british [sic] Garrison will be so important in itself and its consequences, that it must necessarily go a great way towards terminating the war, and securing the invaluable objects of it to the Allies.[21]

Fortunately, Washington prevailed and the operation against Yorktown was brought to a successful conclusion with the surrender of Lord
Cornwallis on October 19, 1781. As George Washington had foreseen, it
was the decisive action of the war.

Although there were no doubt many instances of poor coordination
between our ground and naval forces during the nineteenth century—a
number of "combined" operations were attempted during the Mexican
War of 1848 and during the Civil War—unification of the armed forces
did not become a major issue until the Spanish-American War. The lack
of coordination between the Army and Navy displayed in that conflict,
and the appalling mismanagement of the war effort generally, brought
demands for drastic reforms in the military establishment. Perhaps the
most publicized example of the lack of unified direction was the battle
of Santiago where the capture of the city was delayed for weeks simply
because General Shafter and Admiral Sampson could not agree on a
joint plan of action; and they leaked their disagreements to the press.[22]

As a result of that experience, not only were several steps undertaken to improve the administrative effectiveness of the War and Navy
Departments, but a new Joint Board was created consisting of four
officers from each service, charged with "discussing and reaching common conclusions regarding all matters calling for cooperation of the
two services."[23] The Joint Board, which might be considered the precur-
sor of the Joint Chiefs of Staff, devoted much of its attention to rank,
honors, salutes, etc., and, prior to 1919 when it was reorganized, its ac-
complishments with regard to joint war planning were very limited by
today's standards. During the year and a half that the United States was
an active participant in World War I, the Joint Board met only twice.[24]

World War I was conducted without any significant instances of
friction between the War and Navy Departments. As far as the United
States was concerned, that war was principally a land war, and the
Navy's role was limited, in the main, to protecting the lines of communication across the sea.

Yet in the immediate post-World War I period, there was a great deal
of interest in and discussion of unification of the armed services, a step
never seriously considered before the war. There were two main reasons
for this new interest: first, the high cost of the war which called attention to the need for economy and efficiency; and, second and far more

important, the advent of a new technology—heavier-than-air flight. The airplane, by the very nature of the environment in which it operated, upset the traditional line of demarcation between the jurisdictions of the War and Navy Departments, i.e., land and sea. In addition, the early pioneers of military aviation, led by General Billy Mitchell, made a concerted drive for a separate air service.

It was this demand for a "third" service that focused the discussion on unification and made it an important issue. As Lieutenant Commander (later Admiral) Byrd pointed out to the La Guardia Subcommittee of the House Committee on Military Affairs in the fall of 1919, a third service "... may make close cooperation of the fighting branches of the country more difficult, if not impossible, by creating a third coequal department which must effect far closer cooperation with the other two departments, than these two have ever been able to effect in the past."[25]

A separate air force was violently opposed by the Navy, and almost as violently by the nonflying elements of the Army. In spite of numerous congressional committee hearings in the early 1920's on a separate air force and on unification, and in spite of the introduction of at least sixty unification bills in Congress, little happened except that the old Joint Board was reconstituted with a planning staff, and two new joint committees were established—an Aeronautical Board and an Army-Navy Munitions Board. In 1926, the Army Air Corps was given a significant degree of autonomy within the War Department.[26] By then everyone was exhausted by the controversy, and further unification legislation was delayed two decades—until 1947.

It is interesting to note that as late as 1935 the manual on "Joint Action of the Army and the Navy" still called for each service to be organized and equipped so that it could accomplish its peculiar mission independently of the other, e.g., the Army should have its own sea transports and the Navy, its own land-based aircraft. And as late as 1938, the "Joint Action" manual still declared that "operations of Army and Navy forces will normally be coordinated by mutual cooperation," reserving unified command of joint operations for special agreement between the Secretaries of the Departments or when ordered by the President.[27] Indeed, the doctrine of "mutual cooperation" survived until December 1941, when it was buried in the wreckage of Pearl Harbor.

It was the Second World War, in which combined land/sea/air operations played such a vital role, that finally cracked the opposition to unification, at least with respect to planning and operations. The Joint Chiefs of Staff organization was born during that war, with broader purposes than the old Joint Board; and unified commands were established, although full legislative sanction for these changes had to await the National Security Act of 1947. (A unified command has a continuing mission, a single commander, and consists of elements of two or more services, e.g., the European Command, the North American Air Defense Command, etc.) The Army Air Corps was represented on the Joint Chiefs of Staff and joined with Army and Navy as a virtual equal in the formulation of joint plans. But the JCS could act only by unanimous consent, a procedure which often leads to compromises that are decidedly inferior to the views of any member. By 1943 the Army, led by General Marshall, had accepted the principle of a unified defense establishment—although the Navy definitely had not.

After much study and discussion within the Executive Branch, President Truman, in December 1945, proposed to the Congress a single Department of National Defense, headed by a Secretary of Cabinet rank and supported by an Under Secretary and several Assistant Secretaries. The Department was to comprise three coordinate branches— land forces, naval forces, and air forces—each under an Assistant Secretary. Each branch was to have a military commander, and these three military commanders, together with the Chief of Staff of the Department of National Defense, were to constitute an advisory body to the Secretary of National Defense and to the President. President Truman's plan also provided for unified, centralized common service organizations under either civilian or military leadership in order to "ensure that real unification is ultimately obtained."

The central purpose of President Truman's proposal was to provide for "unified direction of the land, sea, and air forces at home as well as in all other parts of the world where our armed forces are serving." In order to achieve this purpose, he felt that "we should have integrated strategic plans and a unified military program and budget." In this connection he stressed a principle which I believe is only now being generally accepted in the Defense Department, namely, and I use his words, that "strategy, program, and budget are all aspects of the same basic decisions." His plan also stressed the economies that could be achieved through the unification of supply and service functions, the need for strong civilian control, and the requirement for unity of command in outlying bases.[28]

The President's plan was generally favored by the Army but opposed by the Navy.[29] The law which finally evolved after another year and a half of discussion was very different from the one President Truman had proposed. It provided for the creation of a National Military Establishment headed by a Secretary of Defense and comprising three separately organized and administered executive departments—Army, Navy, and Air Force—retaining in these departments "all powers and duties relating to such Departments not specifically conferred upon the Secretary of Defense." The law also provided for the establishment of the Joint Chiefs of Staff, supported by a Joint Staff, and for various boards and committees. In effect, the National Security Act of 1947 established not a unified department or even a federation, but a confederation of three military departments presided over by a Secretary of Defense with carefully enumerated powers.[30]

It is an irony of history that one of the men who most vehemently and effectively opposed President Truman's proposals for a truly unified Department of Defense was destined to be the first to head the new National Military Establishment. Mr. Forrestal, an extremely able and experienced public servant, destroyed his health while trying to make this loose confederation of three military departments work. Within little more than a year, Secretary Forrestal (in his first annual report) was recommending that "the statutory authority of the Secretary of Defense should be materially strengthened . . . by making it clear that the Secretary of Defense has the responsibility for exercising 'direction, authority, and control' over the departments and agencies of the National Military Establishment."[31] (Note the similarity in tone to Secretary of War Root's 1902 proposals with respect to the War Department.) The 1947 Act had authorized the Secretary to establish only "general" policies and programs and to exercise "general" direction, authority, and control. Secretary Forrestal also recommended that the Secretary of Defense be the only representative of the National Military Establishment to sit on the National Security Council. Under the 1947 Act, the Service Secretaries were not only members of the Council but were Heads of Executive Departments as well.

These and other recommendations from Secretary Forrestal, the Hoover Commission, and others, were incorporated in the 1949 Amendments to the National Security Act.[32] The primacy of the Secretary of Defense as the principal assistant to the President on defense matters was stressed. The Army, the Navy, and the Air Force lost their status as executive departments and all that went with it. The Secretary of Defense was given a Deputy and three Assistant Secretaries, a Chairman was provided for the JCS, and the Joint Staff was increased from 100 to 210 officers. And, finally, Title IV was added to the Act creating the Office of the Assistant Secretary of Defense, Comptroller, and providing for uniform budget and fiscal procedures throughout the Department.

On June 30, 1953, Defense's top management was again reorganized.[33] The old statutory agencies, the Munitions Board and the Research and Development Board, were abolished and their functions transferred to the Secretary of Defense whose own office was expanded from three Assistant Secretaries to nine. In transmitting this reorganization plan to the Congress, the President made it clear that *no* function was to be carried out independently of the Secretary of Defense and that the Secretaries of the military departments were to be his "operating managers" in addition to being heads of their own respective departments.[34]

The latest chapter in the history of defense unification legislation was written after Sputnik, in 1958, when the Act was again amended to increase further the responsibilities and authority of the Secretary of Defense, especially with regard to the operational direction of the armed forces and in the research and development area.[35] The three military departments were no longer to be "separately administered" and instead were only to be "separately organized." A new post of Director, Defense Research and Engineering was created, not only to "supervise" research and development activities, but to "direct and control" those activities needing centralized management. Also in the 1958 reorganization the military departments, which had been acting as executive agents in the operational control of the unified and specified commands, were taken out of the command chain, so that the line of command now runs from the President to the Secretary of Defense through the Joint Chiefs of

Staff to the unified commands. And, finally, to enable it to carry out its enlarged functions, the Joint Staff was strengthened further from 210 to 400 officers.

As President Eisenhower pointed out at the time:

... complete unity in our strategic planning and basic operational direction [is a vital necessity]. It is therefore mandatory that the initiative for this planning and direction rest not with the separate services but directly with the Secretary of Defense and his operational advisers, the Joint Chiefs of Staff, assisted by such staff organization as they deem necessary.

No military task is of greater importance than the development of strategic plans which relate our revolutionary new weapons and force deployments to national security objectives. Genuine unity is indispensable at this starting point. No amount of subsequent coordination can eliminate duplication or doctrinal conflicts which are intruded into the first shaping of military programs.[36]

These changes greatly enhanced the authority of the Secretary of Defense as the true operating head of the Defense Department. But it was not until 1961 that the full powers of the Secretary of Defense to run the Department on a unified basis were actually used.

I imply no disrespect to the predecessors of the present Secretary of Defense when I say that although we have now had unification "in name" for almost eighteen years, there was little unification "in fact" until 1961, except in three areas:

1. Unified commands had been created in all overseas theaters and for continental air defense—unified before the beginning of hostilities for the first time in history. But we still do not have a unified command for our strategic retaliatory forces.

2. Joint contingency plans for the use of existing forces had been prepared by the Joint Chiefs of Staff for many contingencies. This had been a strictly military function, with little participation by the civilian Secretaries, but the planning was joint. However, again, there was no joint plan for the targeting of our strategic retaliatory forces until Secretary Gates in 1959/1960 established the mechanism for achieving one. And the plan that was achieved, although joint, was originally a single plan with little in the way of options.

3. Finally, the civilian Secretaries had taken control of the over-all level of the defense budget and brought it into line with the fiscal policy

of the administration. The primary method of so bringing the defense budget into line, used by all Secretaries before the present incumbent, was to divide a total defense budget ceiling among the three military departments, leaving to each department, by and large, the allocation of its ceiling among its own functions, units, and activities. The Defense Secretaries used this method because they lacked the management techniques needed to do it any other way.

In view of these shortcomings President Kennedy, before he took office, was inclined to believe that some further changes in the organization of the Defense Department would be required to improve its effectiveness and make it more responsive to national security objectives and changes in technology. And his Committee on the Defense Establishment, chaired by Senator Symington and including such old defense hands as Thomas Finletter, Roswell Gilpatric and Marx Leva, did indeed propose such changes. The Committee's proposals, aimed at achieving unification in fact as well as form, would have replaced the three Service Secretaries with three Under Secretaries of Defense, vesting directly in the Secretary of Defense the administration of the services. The Chairman of the Joint Chiefs of Staff would have replaced the Joint Chiefs in the chain of command, and the Chiefs would have remained solely as heads of their respective services, their advisory job being assumed by a Military Advisory Council under the Chairman.[37] But the management innovations introduced in the Department of Defense during 1961–62 made unnecessary so drastic an overhaul of the existing organizational structure. What they are and how they have been applied will be the subjects of my next two lectures.

II | Planning—Programming—Budgeting

I NOTED toward the close of my first lecture that although unification had been achieved in form with the passage of the National Security Act in 1947, it was not until 1961 that the full powers of the Secretary of Defense to run the Department on a unified basis—spelled out by various amendments in the intervening years—were actually used. And I suggested that this situation existed principally because earlier Secretaries of Defense lacked the necessary tools to do so.

We have seen how, during the first century of our history under the Constitution, the organization of the defense establishment adjusted itself to its growing task as our national security objectives expanded and our industrial capacity and military technology advanced. We have seen how, by the end of the nineteenth century, new techniques had to be devised to unify the efforts within each of the two military departments, and how some new mechanism had to be created to coordinate the activities of the military services in the conduct of war.

Still, the problems of defense at the close of the nineteenth century were, in retrospect, relatively simple. Although U.S. military forces were employed abroad in limited numbers prior to 1917, it was not until World War I that the United States abandoned George Washington's caution to avoid involvement in the quarrels of Europe. At the close of that War, we again tried to withdraw to our own hemisphere, but some twenty years later we found ourselves even more deeply embroiled in the deteriorating affairs of both Europe and Asia. Since the end of World War II, we have acknowledged and accepted our unavoidable role as a world power and our national security objectives today have been broadened to include the leadership of the collective defense of the entire Free World.

Thus, from a modest beginning, limited to the protection of our land frontiers against the Indians and our neighbors in Florida and Canada, our national security objectives have expanded to involve us in an interlocking system of Free World military alliances with over forty sovereign nations. We now maintain for this purpose by far the largest peacetime establishment in our history. We have, today, a force of almost 2,700,000 military personnel on active duty, supported by about 900,000 civilians in the United States and about one-quarter of a million overseas, the latter mostly citizens of other countries. In addition, we have almost one million reserve personnel and about one-half million retired military personnel on our payrolls.

Pay alone accounts for more than $20 billion out of a total defense budget of $50 billion. The remaining $30 billion is used to procure a staggeringly large variety of goods and services from the private sector of the economy—aircraft, missiles, tanks, food, clothing, research and development, construction and utilities. We draw from virtually every segment of the American economy and utilize a very large share of the Nation's total research and development capacities. Because of the vast scope of our activities—on the land, on and under the seas, in the air and in space—and the great demands we make on our weapons and equipment, the Defense Department is vitally interested in virtually every field of scientific and technological knowledge. The value of our current inventory of equipment, weapons, and supplies is conservatively estimated at $135 billion. Our principal installations and facilities number in the thousands, and we control nearly 15,000 square miles of land. Our military operations extend around the world, and we spend almost $3 billion a year in other countries.

How, one might ask, can any one man or group of men ever hope to manage such a vast aggregation of men, equipment, installations, and activities spread all over the globe? And yet, as we have seen, the defense effort, to be fully effective, must be managed on a unified basis, not only in the conduct of combat operations but also in the planning and execution of the programs. And, as President Eisenhower stressed in 1958: "It is . . . mandatory that the *initiative* for this planning and direction rest not with the separate services but directly with the Secretary of Defense and his operational advisors. . . ."[1]

The revolution in military technology since the end of World War II, alone, would make necessary the central planning and direction of the military program. The great technical complexity of modern day weapons, their lengthy period of development, their tremendous combat power and enormous cost have placed an extraordinary premium on sound choices of major weapon systems. These choices have become, for the top management of the Defense Department, the key decisions around which much else of the defense program revolves. They cannot be made properly by any subordinate echelon of the defense establishment. They must be directly related to our *national* security objectives rather than simply to the tasks of just one of the military services.

The revolution in military technology has not only changed the character of our military program, it has also, to a significant degree, blurred the lines of demarcation among the various services. Is the missile an unmanned aircraft, as the Air Force likes to think, or extended-range artillery, which is the Army view? Most of our major military missions today require the participation of more than one of the military services. Therefore, our principal concern now must be centered on what is required by the defense establishment as a whole to perform a particular military mission—not on what is required by a particular service to perform its part of that mission. This is not only true with regard to the planning of our military forces and programs, but also with respect to the development of new major weapon systems.

I noted in my first lecture that because, prior to 1961, the Defense Secretaries lacked the tools to manage the over-all effort on a truly unified basis, they had to resort (except in times of emergency, like Korea) to what might be described, generically, as the "budget ceiling" approach. The President would indicate the general level of defense expenditures which he felt was appropriate to the international situation and his over-all economic and fiscal policies.[2] The Secretary of Defense, by one means or another, would allocate this figure among the three military departments. Each military department would in turn prepare its basic budget submission, allocating its ceiling among its own functions, units, and activities, and present additional requests, which could not be accommodated within the ceiling, in what was variously called an "addendum" budget, "B" list, etc. Then all the budget submissions were reviewed together by the Office of the Secretary of Defense in an attempt to achieve balance.

Let me make quite clear the fact that this was indeed the traditional way of preparing the defense budget. Frank Pace, then Director of the Bureau of the Budget, in testifying before a congressional committee in 1949 on how the defense budget was prepared in the Truman Administration, described the process as follows:

> We [the Bureau of the Budget] would provide him [the President] with certain factual information as to where certain policies would lead. From that the President sets a ceiling on the armed services, which was last year, I think, generally known as $15 billion.
>
> However, I think it sould be explained that under the ceiling process—and this is not solely for the armed forces but exists for every department of the Government— ...
>
> There is also the proviso that if within that limitation it is impossible to include certain programs which the Secretary of Defense considers of imperative importance to the national defense, they shall be included in ... what is termed the "B" list. ... The "B" list is what cannot be included under the ceiling.[3]

It was recognized long ago that this was a rather inefficient way to go about preparing the defense budget. Its consequences were precisely what could have been predicted. Each service tended to exercise its own priorities, favoring its own unique missions to the detriment of joint missions, striving to lay the groundwork for an increased share of the budget in future years by concentrating on alluring new weapon systems, and protecting the over-all size of its own forces even at the cost of readiness. These decisions were made by patriotic generals and admirals, and by dedicated civilian leaders as well, who were convinced that they were acting in the best interests of the Nation as well as of their own service—but the end result was not balanced effective military forces.

The Air Force, for example, gave overriding priority to the strategic retaliatory bombers and missiles, starving the tactical air units needed to support the Army ground operations and the airlift units needed to move our limited war forces quickly to far-off trouble spots. The Navy gave overriding priority to its own nuclear attack forces—notably the aircraft carriers—while its antisubmarine warfare capability was relatively neglected and its escort capability atrophied. The Army used its limited resources to preserve the number of its divisions, although this meant that they lacked equipment and supplies to fight for more than a few weeks.

Moreover, because attention was focused on only the next fiscal year, the services had every incentive to propose large numbers of "new starts," the full cost dimensions of which would only become apparent in subsequent years. This is the "foot in the door" or "thin edge of the wedge" technique which the one-year-at-a-time approach to defense budgeting greatly encouraged.

Another unsatisfactory aspect of this method of attempting to exercise control and direction of the defense effort through the annual budget was the almost complete separation between budgeting and military planning. (I speak here of medium and long-range planning, including weapon systems planning—not the contingency planning for the use of existing forces to which I referred in my first lecture.)

1. These critically important functions were performed by two different groups of people—the planning by the military planners and the budgeting by the civilian Secretaries and the comptroller organizations.

2. Budget control was exercised by the Secretary of Defense but planning remained essentially in the services. It was not until 1955–56 that the first Joint Strategic Objectives Plan (JSOP), projecting the requirements for major forces some four to five years into the future, was prepared by the Joint Chiefs of Staff organization, but the early JSOP was essentially a "pasting together" of unilaterally developed service plans.

3. Whereas the planning horizon extended four or more years into the future, the budget was projected only one year ahead, although it was clear to all involved that the lead time from the start of a weapon development to the equipping of the forces ranged from five to ten years, depending on the character of the particular development effort.

4. Planning was performed in terms of missions, weapon systems, and military units or forces—the "outputs" of the Defense Department; budgeting, on the other hand, was done in terms of such "inputs" or intermediate products as personnel, operation and maintenance, procurement, construction, etc.; and there was little or no machinery for translating one into the other.

5. Budgeting, however crudely, faced up to fiscal realities. The planning was fiscally unrealistic and, therefore, of little help to the decision-maker. The total implicit budget costs of the unilateral service plans or of the Joint Strategic Objectives Plan always far exceeded any budget that any Secretary of Defense or administration was willing to request of the Congress.

6. Military requirements tended to be stated in absolute terms, without reference to their costs. But the military effectiveness or military worth of any given weapon system cannot logically be considered in isolation. It must be considered in relation to its cost—and, in a world in which resources are limited, to the alternative uses to which the resources can be put. Military requirements are meaningful only in terms of benefits to be gained in relation to their cost. Accordingly, resource costs and military worth have to be scrutinized together.

As a consequence, the Secretary each year found himself in a position where he had, at least implicitly, to make major decisions on forces and programs without adequate information and all within the few weeks allocated to his budget review. Moreover, every year the plans and programs of each of the services had to be cut back severely to fit the budget ceiling, by program cancellations, stretch-outs, or postponements—but only for that year. Beyond the budget year, unrealistic plans continued to burgeon—perhaps next year the ceiling would be higher.

These deficiencies did not go unnoticed in the Congress. Representative George Mahon, then Chairman of the House Defense Appropriations Subcommittee and now also Chairman of the full Committee, addressed two letters to the Secretary of Defense in the summer and fall of 1959. In his first letter he stressed the importance of looking at the defense program and budget in terms of major military missions, by grouping programs and their cost by mission.[4] In his second letter, he called "for more useful information and for a practical means of relating costs to missions."[5]

Many other students of the defense management problem had reached the same conclusion, including the group with which I had the honor to be associated at the RAND Corporation. Many of these conclusions found their way into a book, *The Economics of Defense in the Nuclear Age*,[6] which was published for the RAND corporation in March 1960, some ten months before I was called upon as Assistant Secretary of Defense (Comptroller) to help introduce them into the Defense Department.

The new Secretary of Defense, Robert S. McNamara, made it clear from the beginning that he intended to be the kind of Secretary that President Eisenhower had in mind in 1958 and take the initiative in the planning and direction of the defense program. In a television interview, after having been in office less than one month, Secretary McNamara defined his managerial philosophy as follows:

I think that the role of public manager is very similar to the role of a private manager; in each case he has the option of following one of two major alternative courses of action. He can either act as a judge or a leader. In the former case, he sits and waits until subordinates bring to him problems for solution, or alternatives for choice. In the latter case, he immerses himself in the operations of the business or the governmental activity, examines the problems, the objectives, the alternative courses of action, chooses among them, and leads the organization to their accomplishment. In the one case, it's a passive role; in the other case, an active role. . . . I have always believed in and endeavored to follow the active leadership role as opposed to the passive judicial role.[7]

Furthermore, Secretary McNamara made it known that he wanted to manage the defense effort in terms of meaningful program entities— of "outputs" like the B-52 force, the POLARIS force, the Army Airborne Division force, etc., associating with each output all the inputs of equipment, personnel, supplies, facilities, and funds, regardless of the appropriation account in which each was financed. He wanted to know and, indeed, would have to know in order to optimize the allocation of resources, the cost of, for example, a B-52 wing—not only the cost of equipping the wing but also the cost of manning and operating it for its lifetime or at least for a reasonable period of years in the future. Only then would he be in a position to assess the cost and effectiveness of a B-52 wing as compared with other systems designed to perform the same or similar tasks.

Moreover, he wanted to know the total costs of the forces assigned to each of the major missions—the costs of the strategic offensive forces, the continental defense forces, the general purpose forces, etc. As General Maxwell Taylor had pointed out to a congressional committee in 1960:

... If we are called upon to fight, we will not be interested in the services as such. We will be interested rather in task forces, those combinations of Army, Navy, and Air Force which are functional in nature, such as the atomic retaliatory forces, overseas deployments, continental air defense forces, limited war expeditionary forces, and the like. But the point is that we do not keep our budget in these terms. Hence it is not an exaggeration to say that we do not know what kind and how much defense we are buying with any specific budget.[8]

These views closely coincided with my own. The Secretary and I both realized that the financial management system of the Defense Department must serve many purposes. It must produce a budget in a form acceptable to the Congress. It must account for the funds in the same manner in which they were appropriated. It must provide the managers at all levels in the defense establishment the financial information they need to do their particular jobs in an effective and economical manner. It must produce the financial information required by other agencies of the government—the Bureau of the Budget, the Treasury, and the General Accounting Office.

But we both were convinced that the financial management system must also provide the data needed by top defense management to make the really crucial decisions, particularly on the major forces and weapon systems needed to carry out the principal missions of the defense establishment. And we were well aware that the financial management system, as it had evolved over the years, could not directly produce the required data in the form desired. It was clear that a new function, which we call programming, would have to be incorporated in the financial management system. I had hoped that I would have at least a year to smooth the way for the introduction of this new function. I recall outlining the proposed programming system to Secretary McNamara in the spring of 1961 and recommending that we spend eighteen months developing and installing it, beginning in the first year with a limited number of trial programs, with a view to expanding the system to include all programs during 1962. The Secretary approved the proposed system but shortened my timetable from eighteen months to six. Somehow we developed and installed it, Department-wide, in time to use it as a basis for the fiscal year 1963 defense budget. Submitted to Congress in January 1962, this was the first budget to be prepared wholly under the new administration.

Since the military planning function and the budget function were already well established, the role of programming was to provide a bridge between the two. It was, of course, theoretically possible to recast both the planning and budget structures in terms of major programs related to missions. In fact, the military planning operation was later adapted to the program structure, and I once thought that the budget structure should be similarly realigned. You will find on page 56 of *The Economics of Defense in the Nuclear Age* a format for such a program budget.

But the existing budget structure serves some very useful purposes. It is organized, essentially, in terms of resource categories: (1) Military Personnel; (2) Operation and Maintenance; (3) Procurement; (4) Research, Development, Test and Evaluation; and (5) Military Construction.

This type of structure lends itself ideally to the manner in which the Defense Department actually manages its resources. Although military planning and the formulation of programs should logically be done in terms of missions and forces, the Department must be managed not only in those terms but also in terms of resources. For example, we have to manage the acquisition, training, and careers of military personnel; the operation of bases and facilities; the procurement of aircraft, missiles, ships, and tanks; the research and development program; and the construction of airfields, missile sites, quarters, and other additions to our existing physical plant. The present budget structure facilitates the estimation of resource costs as well as the execution of the resource programs.

This division of the budget by broad input or resource categories also provides needed flexibility for the adjustments in the program that are inevitably required in the course of the budget year. Program priorities and requirements always change in unanticipated ways even in the course of a single year as a result of international developments, technological breakthroughs (or disappointments), and all sorts of other events. It is important not to freeze programs in appropriation bills.

Finally, the Congress, and particularly the Appropriations Committees, prefer the existing arrangement of the defense budget.[9] They have been working with it for more than a decade and have established an historical basis for forming judgments on the validity of the budget requests. It is much easier for an Appropriations Committee, for example, to review a budget request of $4.3 billion for pay and allowances for 960,000 active duty Army personnel than, say, a request of $18 or $19 billion for the major program "General Purpose Forces," or even a request of $700 million for the program element "Army Infantry Divisions." Although the President, under the Budget and Accounting Act of 1921, can propose his budget in any form he pleases, it is the Congress that determines how the funds will be appropriated and this, in turn, determines how the funds will be accounted for. I now feel that the advantages of the existing budget structure far outweigh the disadvantages, which are principally mechanical, namely, the need to translate program categories into budget categories and vice versa. This is the sort of disadvantage that modern high-speed computers are well designed to overcome.

Accordingly, we decided to leave the budget structure undisturbed and to span the gap between planning and budgeting with the new programming function. This resulted in a three-phase operation: planning-programming-budgeting.

The first phase—military planning and requirements determination—we envisioned as a continuing year-round operation involving the participation of all appropriate elements of the Defense Department in their respective areas of responsibility. We anticipated that the Joint Chiefs of Staff organization and the planners in the military departments would play a particularly important role in this phase. What we were looking for here were not just requirement studies in the traditional sense, but military-economic studies which compared alternative ways of accomplishing national security objectives and which tried to determine the one that contributes the most for a given cost or achieves a given objective at the least cost. These are what we call "cost-effectiveness studies" or systems analyses, and they are the subject of my third lecture.

I had originally thought that once an approved five-year program had been developed, the Joint Chiefs of Staff organization and the military planners in the departments would concentrate their attention on specific segments of the program which might require change, and that they would propose such changes whenever the need became apparent any time during the year. When these change proposals were approved, the five-year program would be modified accordingly, thereby providing an up-to-date long-range plan at all times. But I had given too little weight to the need to review and analyze, at least once a year, the entire long-range program in all of its interrelated parts, rather than in bits and pieces during the course of the entire year. I must confess that the Joint Chiefs of Staff saw this need more clearly than I did. They wanted to make a comprehensive program review each year to take account of the latest changes in military technology and in the international situation; so did each of the military departments; and so did the Secretary.

Accordingly, the planning-programming-budgeting process now starts with the Joint Strategic Objectives Plan prepared by the Joint Chiefs of Staff organization with the help of the military planners in the services. As I noted earlier, the format of this plan has been modified to bring it into harmony with the new program structure. Thus, the Joint Chiefs of Staff have the opportunity each year to recommend to the Secretary of Defense on a comprehensive basis the military forces and major programs which they believe should be supported over the next five to eight years. The Secretary of Defense in the spring of each year reviews these recommended forces and programs, makes preliminary decisions, and provides to the military departments what is called "tentative force guidance" to serve as a basis for the preparation of their formal change proposals to the official five-year program. The principal "cost-effectiveness" studies are scheduled for completion at about the same time in order to provide the Secretary and his principal advisors with information in depth on the most critical and difficult requirement problems.

I recall that the first list of these requirements projects was developed by Secretary McNamara and were known at the time as "McNamara's 100 trombones." These projects were assigned to the Joint Chiefs of Staff, the military departments, and various elements of the Office of the Secretary of Defense. One, for example, dealt with the question of how many strategic bombers and missiles we would need during the next decade to destroy priority targets. Another involved an examination of requirements for airlift and sealift to meet various contingency war plans and the most economical means of providing that lift. Still another dealt with the comparative advantages and costs of: (1) refurbishing existing items of ground equipment, (2) replacing them with new equipment off the assembly lines, and (3) expediting the development of still better equipment. The Secretary of Defense still originates many of these requirements studies. Others are originated by the Joint Chiefs of Staff, the military departments, and various elements of the Secretary's staff.

The initial development of the programming system, the second phase, was an enormous undertaking, considering the short time allowed and the fact that we had to handle simultaneously three amendments to the fiscal year 1962 budget originally prepared by the preceding administration. The problem here was to sort out all of the myriad programs and activities of the defense establishment and regroup them into meaningful program elements, i.e., integrated combinations of men, equipment, and installations whose effectiveness could be related to our national security objectives. These are the basic building blocks as well as the decision-making levels of the programming process. As I noted earlier, the B-52 bomber force, together with all of the supplies, weapons, and manpower needed to make it militarily effective is one such program element. Other examples are Attack Carriers, F-4 Fighter Wings, the Manned Orbiting Laboratory development project, and Recruit Training. Wherever possible, program elements are measured in physical terms such as numbers of aircraft per wing, numbers of operational missiles on launchers, numbers of active ships, and so forth as well as in financial terms, thus including both "input" and "output"—costs and benefits. Of course, such program elements as research projects can only be measured in terms of inputs.

Costs are measured in terms of what we call "total obligational authority"—the amount required to finance the program element in a given year, regardless of when the funds are appropriated by the Congress, obligated, placed on contract, or spent. Now, admittedly, this is something of a compromise.[10] It would be preferable to cost the program in terms of expenditures; or, ideally, in terms of resources consumed. However, the accounting difficulties appeared so great that we did not attempt that approach. Moreover, as long as the budget is in terms of obligational authority, the program must be, for the program has to be firmly anchored to the budget. We do not even find it necessary to cost individual program elements in terms of cash expenditures. We have a much better idea of the full cost of 100 MINUTEMAN missiles, for example, than of the phasing of the actual expenditures year by year. And from the point of view of planning and decision-making we are far more interested in the full cost of a program—in "cost to complete"—than in the precise phasing of the costs.

To tie in with the "branch points" at which critical decisions must be made, we subdivide program costs into three categories: development costs, investment costs, and operating costs. Because of the great expense involved in just developing a new weapon system to the point where it could be produced and deployed, a determination to go ahead with full-scale development is, in itself, a major decision. There are few major weapon system developments today that can be accomplished for less than $1 billion. For example, we will have spent $1.5 billion making two prototypes of the B-70. We have already spent $1.5 billion developing the NIKE-ZEUS anti-ballistic missile system and are now spending a comparable amount on the NIKE X. We spent $2.3 billion developing the ATLAS ICBM, $2.6 billion on TITAN, $2.5 billion on POLARIS, and $2.1 billion on MINUTEMAN I. Even the development of a new torpedo can cost as much as $75 million. Therefore, we need to know in advance the likely cost of completing any major weapon development.

Obviously, before we go ahead with the next phase, production and deployment, we need to know the investment cost of providing initial equipment for the proposed forces. And, finally, we need to know the cost of operating the proposed forces each year. In many cases, for example a B-52 wing, the five-year operating costs are about equal to the initial equipment costs, and in some few cases, for example an infantry division, the operating costs for just one year are actually greater than the initial investment costs.

To facilitate the conversion of program costs to the budget and vice versa, we also had to break down the costs of each program element by the various budget appropriation accounts in which it is financed. Operating costs typically are financed in the "Military Personnel" and "Operation and Maintenance" appropriations and, where operating spares are involved, in the "Procurement" accounts as well. Initial investment costs typically are financed in the "Procurement" and "Military Construction" appropriations.

We have nearly 1,000 program elements. Where military forces are involved, they are projected eight years ahead in order to provide the necessary lead time for the determination of the procurement programs. All other program data, both physical and financial, are projected five years ahead. For purposes of continuity, all program data are shown for each year beginning in fiscal year 1962; thus, our present Five-Year Force Structure and Financial Program extends from fiscal year 1962 through fiscal year 1970, with forces projected through fiscal year 1973. The entire program is subject to continual change and is, therefore, updated every other month. Whenever a change is made in the cost of a program element in the current fiscal year, it must also be reflected in the budget for the same year and vice versa. Considering the vast quantities of data involved in the planning-programming-budgeting system, the only practical solution was to transfer the entire operation to a computer system. This we have now accomplished.

The next task was to relate the program elements to the major missions of the Defense Department. The objective here was to assemble related groups of program elements that, for decision purposes, should be considered together either because they supported one another or because they were close substitutes. The unifying principle underlying each major program is a common mission or set of purposes for the elements involved. We now have nine major programs:

1. Strategic Retaliatory Forces
2. Continental Defense Forces
3. General Purpose Forces
4. Airlift and Sealift
5. Reserve and Guard
6. Research and Development
7. General Support
8. Retired Pay
9. Military Assistance

The Strategic Retaliatory Forces program includes the manned bomber forces, the land-based missile forces, the sea-based missile forces, and related headquarters and command support activities. Within the aircraft forces are the B-52 long-range bombers together with their air-to-ground HOUND DOG missiles and QUAIL decoy missiles, the B-58 and B-47 medium bombers, and the refueling tankers. Within the missile forces are the ATLAS, TITAN, and MINUTEMAN ICBM's and the POLARIS submarine-launched missiles. Also included in the Strategic Retaliatory Forces are the SR-71 and other strategic reconnaissance aircraft and the special communication links and control systems, such as the Post Attack Command and Control System aircraft, which are required for the effective direction of these forces.

The Continental Defense Forces, which might be called the strategic defensive forces, include the North American surveillance, warning, and control network, consisting of land-based, sea-based, and airborne radars and control centers; the manned interceptors; the surface-to-air missiles; the ballistic missile warning systems; the antisatellite defense systems; and the civil defense program.

All of the forces in these two major programs would come into play in a general nuclear war. And, as a matter of interest, we have, during the last year, broadened our analyses to treat all of these forces simultaneously in the context of a general nuclear war. This is important because the strategic offensive forces also make a contribution to the "damage limiting" mission, which is the principal purpose of the Continental Defense Forces. A portion of our strategic offensive forces can be applied against an enemy's strategic offensive forces, thus reducing under certain circumstances the potential weight of his attack.

The third, and the largest, major program is that for the General Purpose Forces. These are the forces designed to fight local or limited wars and to engage in theater operations in general war. This major program is organized broadly along service lines. Within the service breakdowns, the basic identifiable combat units form the program elements. Army General Purpose Forces include almost all of the regular combat units and command support elements. They range from the four basic kinds of divisions—infantry, armor, mechanized, and airborne—through the missile commands to artillery battalions, air defense units for the field army, and aviation companies.

The Navy's list is even longer, embracing all of the combatant ships and support vessels except for the strategic missile firing submarines, the radar warning picket ships, and the Military Sea Transportation Service ships. All of the Fleet's various aircraft units are also included except, of course, those assigned to airborne early warning as part of the continental defense system. Components of Navy General Purpose Forces include the carrier and antisubmarine warfare forces.

All Marine Corps units are listed under General Purpose Forces, including the Marine aircraft wings.

The Air Force General Purpose Forces consist principally of those units assigned to the Tactical Air Command in the United States and to the theater commands overseas. The tactical fighters and bombers, tactical reconnaissance aircraft, and the MACE missiles, and their associated command and control systems and headquarters, all fall within this category.

The fourth major program is that for Airlift and Sealift. The troop carrier wings of the Air Force, including theater airlift, the Military Air Transport Service aircraft, and the Military Sea Transportation Service ships, make up the essential components of this group.

The fifth major program is composed of the Reserve and National Guard Forces. The program elements are arranged by service and by the major mission each element or unit supports. Actually, Reserve and National Guard program elements are reviewed as parts of the appropriate mission packages—Continental Defense Forces, General Purpose Forces, Airlift and Sealift Forces, and so forth, as well as in the context of the reserve components themselves. This is a case where for decision purposes we want visibility both ways—as reserve components and as parts of mission forces.

The sixth major program, Research and Development, includes all of the R&D projects which are not directly associated with program elements in other major programs. The R&D program elements are grouped into four categories, ranging from pencil pushing to operational hardware:

1. Research—the effort directed toward the expansion of knowledge of natural phenomena and our environment and the solution of problems in the physical, biological, medical, behavioral, social, and engineering sciences.

2. Exploratory Developments—the effort directed toward the expansion of technological knowledge and the development of materials, components, devices, and subsystems which it is hoped will have some useful application to new military weapons and equipment. Here the emphasis is on exploring the feasibility of new ideas, up to the point of demonstration with "breadboard" devices and prototype components and subsystems.

3. Advanced Developments—the effort directed toward the development of experimental hardware for technical or operational testing of its suitability for military purposes, prior to the determination of whether the item should be designed or engineered for actual service use. Here is where we begin to identify each project with a specific military application or technique, and we begin to question in depth its potential military utility. During this phase we also begin to explore the costs of the most likely applications in order to determine whether the potential operational benefit would be worth the cost of development, production, and deployment.

4. Engineering Developments—the effort directed toward the development of a particular system engineered for service use and for operational employment, but which has not as yet been approved for production and deployment. It is at this point that large commitments of resources must be made to single projects. Accordingly, before full-scale development is initiated, the specific operational requirements and the cost-effectiveness of the system must be confirmed, and goals, milestones, and time schedules must be established.

Operational Systems Developments—the effort directed toward the continued development, test, evaluation, and design improvement of projects which have already entered (or have been approved for) the production-deployment stage—are included in other major programs as integral parts of the appropriate program elements. For example, the continuing development of MINUTEMAN II is included in the program element "MINUTEMAN II" under the major program "Strategic Retaliatory Forces."

The seventh major program, General Support, is the "all other" program containing all of the activities not readily allocable to mission forces or weapon systems. Some of its major subcategories are: individual training and education including recruit training, technical training, flight training, and service academies; communications between higher headquarters and Unified Commands; most intelligence collection; medical services; support of higher headquarters; and so forth. In dollar value this is a large category, accounting for almost 30 per cent of the total defense budget. It is essentially the "overhead" of the Defense Department, although much of it, like training, is "variable" overhead.

The eighth major program, Retired Pay, has been separately identified because it represents costs beyond our direct control. The terms of retirement and the rates of pay are established by law. Expenditures for this purpose will amount to $1.5 billion in the next fiscal year and are increasing rapidly as World War II veterans join the retired ranks.

The last major program, Military Assistance, includes the military equipment and training being provided to some fifty-nine foreign nations. For administrative purposes, we have found it best to retain this activity as a separate program.[11]

All of the program data, together with the description of the forces, their tasks and missions, procurement lists, facility lists, and so forth, constitute, collectively, what we term "The Five-Year Force Structure and Financial Program." Since the data are machine processed, they can be summarized in different ways. For the use of top management in the Defense Department we prepare and update at regular intervals a special summary volume which displays in tabular form the forces, financial, manpower, and procurement programs. The Five-Year Force Structure and Financial Program is formally approved by the Secretary of Defense and is binding for programming purposes on all components of the Department.

We recognized from the beginning that the defense program is extremely dynamic and that changes would be required at various times during the year. Accordingly, we established a formal program change control system. The basic elements of this system involve the submission of program change proposals by any major component of the Defense Department, their review by all interested components, the Secretary's decision on each proposal, and finally, the assignment of responsibility for carrying out this particular decision to the appropriate military department or agency. Hundreds of program change proposals are submitted each year requesting changes involving billions of dollars.

This brings us to the third phase of the planning-programming-budgeting process. It may be forth emphasizing at this point that the programming review is not intended as a substitute for the annual budget review. Rather, it is designed to provide a Defense Department-approved program to serve as a basis for the preparation of the annual budget as well as guidance for future planning. In the budget review we go into greater detail, for the next year of the Five-Year Program, on procurement lists, production schedules, lead times, prices, status of funds, and all the other facets involved in the preparation of an annual budget. And, as I pointed out earlier, we still manage our funds in terms of the appropriation accounts as well as in terms of the program structure. Essentially, the annual budget now represents a detailed analysis of the financial requirements of the first annual increment of the approved Five-Year Program.

Thus, we have provided for the Secretary of Defense and his principal military and civilian advisors a system which brings together at one place and at one time all of the relevant information that they need to make sound decisions on the forward program and to control the execution of that program. And we have provided the necessary flexibility in the form of a program change control system. Now, for the first time, the largest business in the world has a comprehensive Defense Department-wide plan that extends more than one year into the future. And it is a realistic and responsible one—programming not only the forces, but also the men, equipment, supplies, installations, and budget dollars required to support them. Budgets are in balance with programs, programs with force requirements, force requirements with military missions, and military missions with national security objectives. And the total budget dollars required by the plan for future years do not exceed the Secretary's responsible opinion of what is necessary and feasible.

With this management tool at his command, the Secretary of Defense is now in a position to carry out the responsibilities assigned to him by the National Security Act, namely, to exercise "direction, authority, and control over the Department of Defense"—and without another major reorganization of the defense establishment.

III | Cost-Effectiveness

MIDWAY in my second lecture I alluded, in connection with the first phase of the planning-programming-budgeting process, to the need for military-economic studies which compare alternative ways of accomplishing national security objectives and which try to determine the way that contributes the most for a given cost or achieves a given objective for the least cost. The extensive and comprehensive use of these "cost-effectiveness" studies or systems analyses was the second major innovation introduced into the decision-making process of the Defense Department.

Although the introduction of the programming function was generally well received, considerable controversy arose over this extensive use of cost-effectiveness studies in the decision-making process, and some of this controversy continues. Why this is so is something of a mystery to me. We have made repeated efforts to explain the essential nature of these studies and the contribution that they make to the achievement of greater military effectiveness as well as economy in the defense establishment. But the suspicion still persists in some influential quarters that, somehow or other, cost-effectiveness studies put "dollars before national security," or will result in our going to war with "cut-rate, cut-quality, cheapest-to-buy weapons."[1] Virtually every attempt we have made to explain the inexorable logic of relating cost to military effectiveness seems to shatter itself on the argument—"Nothing but the best will do for our boys." And the "best" usually refers to some particular characteristic of physical performance, such as speed, altitude, or firepower, or even unit cost!

Implicit in this challenge is the deeply rooted feeling that national defense is far too important a matter to be inhibited by cost. If one weapon system performs better than another, then we should buy the higher performance system, regardless of cost; the country can afford it. Indeed, the people who hold this view feel that it is somehow sinful, or at least unpatriotic, to try to relate performance or military effectiveness to costs; that considerations of military effectiveness and cost are antithetical.

To anyone trained in economics, this is a most puzzling attitude. We know that the very act of making a choice—and that is all we are doing when we choose weapons—involves weighing the utility or benefit to be gained against the cost which must be incurred. Why is that so? It is so because benefits *cost* resources and we live in a world in which resources are limited. If we use more for one purpose, less remains for other purposes—even in as rich a nation as the United States.

Certainly, most of us are continuously being forced to make such choices in our personal lives. Although explicit calculations may be rare in these personal choices, they are common, if not quite universal, in business affairs. Indeed, the weighing of benefits against costs is one of the imperatives of any good business decision. The fact that one machine can produce twice as much or twice as fast as another must obviously be weighed against its additional cost in order to determine which is the more profitable. The principle is exactly the same in defense, except that in private business the manager is guided by the profit goal and the market prices of what he buys and sells; whereas in government the decision-maker, since he is not selling in a market, must determine the worth of his "product," e.g., of added performance, by careful analysis and the application of experienced judgment. In this respect, cost-effectiveness analysis is more difficult in defense than in a private firm operating in a market economy, and even more important.

Contrary to the suspicion in some quarters, the scarcity of resources and the consequent necessity for economic choice is not the invention of economists or defense comptrollers, or even of the Democratic administration. The Hoover Commission in its report of June 1955 pointed out that:

The question of "quantity" cannot be considered except in conjunction with that of "cost." Just as in a business, one cannot make a decision to buy material or equipment without simultaneous consideration of price, so the Government cannot intelligently consider the wisdom of embarking on any program without a similar consideration of its cost. A decision to increase or decrease the number of air wings is intimately connected with consideration of the cost at which an air wing can be equipped and operated.[2]

The role of the cost-effectiveness study is to assist management in making just such decisions by bringing into clearer focus the impact on overall military effectiveness of an increase or decrease in the number of air wings and the specific cost implications of such changes.

I was somewhat startled about a year ago to read a statement by a leading member of the Congress:

There is no hard evidence that the Soviet Union is applying cost-effectiveness criteria in its planning for future weapons systems. In fact, many knowledgeable students of Soviet thinking believe that the opposite is quite probably the case.[3]

It reminded me of a statement made some years earlier by Hanson Baldwin to the effect that:

In the Western World—though not in Russia—costs are a more decisive factor in shaping defense than is military logic.[4]

The idea that the Soviets pay little attention to cost is a very common misconception in this country. At the risk of opening up a new controversy on the "cost-effectiveness gap," let me assure you that the Soviet leaders are most sensitive to the need for applying cost-effectiveness principles in all of their economic planning, and there is no reason to doubt that they follow the same approach in the military area. For example, here is a statement from the program adopted by the 22nd Congress of the Communist Party of the Soviet Union in 1961:

Chief attention in all links of planning and economic management must be focused on the most rational and effective use of material, labor, financial and natural resources, and on the elimination of excessive expenditures and losses. It is an immutable law of economic construction to achieve, in the interests of society, the greatest results at the lowest cost.[5]

The formulation is not elegant, or even accurate, but the sense of it shines through.

That military expenditures were not excluded from this consideration was made evident by Mr. Khrushchev's explanation of the cutback in the Soviet military forces announced in January 1960. At that time he said:

The elimination of nonproductive expenditures and the search for additional possibilities for economic development are tasks that constantly confront not only us but any state. I repeat that this matter is always urgent and will always attract unflagging attention.... The proposal to reduce the Soviet Armed Forces ... will yield an annual saving of approximately 16,000,000,000 to 17,-000,000,000 rubles [old rubles]. This will be a very tangible saving for our people and our country. It represents a powerful reinforcement for fulfilling and over-fulfilling our economic plans.[6]

And as further evidence, the U.S.S.R. has now translated *The Economics of Defense in the Nuclear Age* into Russian, with a first printing of 10,000 copies (but no royalties!).

Thus it seems plain that the Soviets, too, realize that they are not immune to the laws of economics, that they are not exempt from having to choose among the various alternative claims on the limited resources available to them. Nor do they appear reluctant to make use of the most modern methods and techniques to assist their managers in making these choices. Clearly, the Soviets have also realized that the modern world is far too complex to rely solely on intuitive judgment and that their decision-makers must be supported by quantitative analysis.

But opposition to cost-effectiveness studies stems not only from a suspicion of quantitative analysis but also from the conviction—completely unsubstantiated but nevertheless firmly held—that these studies inevitably lead to decisions favoring the cheapest weapon. Nothing could be further from the truth. Cost-effectiveness analysis is completely neutral with respect to the unit cost of a weapon. What it is concerned with is: Which strategy (or force, or weapon system) offers the greatest amount of military effectiveness for a given outlay? Or looking at the problem from another direction: How can a given level of military effectiveness be achieved at least cost?

In some cases the most "economical" weapon may be the one with the highest unit cost; in other cases, it may be the one with the lowest unit cost—it will depend on the relative military worth of quality and quantity in the particular circumstances. Unit cost, by itself, is simply an index—an inverse index—of quantity. There have been many cases in history where the cheaper and technically less efficient weapon proved to be the "best," simply because its lower cost permitted it to be acquired in much greater numbers.

I am indebted to Joseph Alsop for one of the earliest reported cases of this phenomenon. In his book on the Greek Bronze Age, which he calls *From the Silent Earth,*[7] Mr. Alsop puts forth his theory on the collapse of the Mycenaean Greek civilization in about the twelfth century before Christ. The destruction of that civilization was so complete that even the written language was lost and the Greeks remained illiterate until the arrival of the new alphabet about 750 B.C.

The speed and completeness with which the Mycenaeans were virtually wiped off the face of the earth he attributes to the fact that the Dorians invading from the northwest used primitive iron swords against the highly developed bronze weapons of the Mycenaeans. The first of the Mycenaean centers to be destroyed was Pylos on the west coast of Greece, the nearest to the Dorians. Pylian society was much more highly developed than that of the Dorians, and the two evidently engaged in trade. Thus the Pylians were probably aware of iron weapons. Why then did they not make the obvious conversion from bronze to iron? Mr. Alsop suggests two reasons: One, the more advanced Pylians would have been reluctant to believe that a great advance in weaponry could possibly be achieved by their Dorian poor relations; and two, and I quote Mr. Alsop directly:

...unless the Pylian fighting men were very different from any subsequent soldiers, they would have been inclined to pooh-pooh the ugly, gray, innovating blades of the Dorians....

...the earliest iron weapons may not have been immensely better, sword for sword, than the good bronze blades of late Mycenaean times. Some students of the subject have even suggested that at this early stage in iron technology a swordsman must have had to stop and bend his sword back into shape after a few hacks at his enemy. One can all but hear the Pylian senior officers snorting with complacent disdain because of the defects of iron. But . . . the Pylian senior officers would then have failed to notice the essential point—that iron, being common, could be used to arm everyone, instead of being restricted, like bronze, to the armament of a military elite. Whole hordes of iron-armed soldiers would soon overwhelm a smaller, elite, bronze-armed force, even if the individual bronze swords were better than the iron swords.[8]

Bronze, as Mr. Alsop pointed out, was a semi-precious metal at that time, and, as we know from other sources, bronze weapons were relatively expensive to produce. Thus, cost alone could explain why all Bronze Age armies, not only the Pylians, were generally small and based on an elite corps. Here we see how a technically inferior weapon, simply because it is cheaper and therefore can be acquired in larger numbers, can beat the superior weapon which is dear and can only be acquired in small numbers.

But there were other times in history when "quality" appeared to have carried the day. For example, after the Persians, using relatively large armies, carved a major empire for themselves in the fifth century B.C., the Spartans, by concentrating on the training of an elite corps called hoplites, by refining their offensive and defensive weapons, and by using advanced tactical formations—in other words, by emphasizing "quality"—proved the worth of their small but highly effective army against a larger Persian army. The greater effectiveness of the Spartan hoplite over his Persian counterpart lay not only in his training but in his equipment and support as well. Each hoplite was provided with some seventy-two pounds of equipment and was supported by seven helots or serfs who formed the rear ranks, making the phalanx eight deep. Although the investment per hoplite was very high, his great combat effectiveness crowned Spartan arms with success.[9]

After the fall of the Roman Empire, the picture becomes less clear. But by the early Middle Ages, "quality" again emerged as a decisive factor, first with the development of intricate armor plates as a means of protecting the horseman and his horse, and second, with the appearance of the fortified castle. Both of these innovations required tremendous investments, made the individual far more effective for both offense and defense, and led again to reliance on an expensive elite corps. The cost of the armored knight was staggering for those times. By the end of the Middle Ages each knight required upwards of two hundred pounds of hammered plate for himself and his horse, plus a large retinue to keep him in the field. But the armored knight was a highly effective weapon system. It is said that in the eleventh century a force of about seventy knights conquered the ancient and civilized kingdom of Sicily.[10]

Then the pendulum swung to quantity when a new, relatively inexpensive weapon successfully challenged the knight and helped to end the age of feudalism. The Battle of Crécy during the Hundred Years' War pitted the longbowman against the knight and over 1,500 French lords and knights fell as compared to a few dozen English archers.[11] And then the musket and black powder challenged the bow, not because the musket was superior to the bow and arrow; it wasn't. The musket had less range and accuracy than the bow and a much lower rate of fire. But let my colleague Eugene Fubini tell that story:

> The main advantage of the musket was that it was much cheaper to equip troops with musket and powder than with the bow and arrow. Moreover, in the early days, the musket did not require much actual training, because accuracy was not a factor. Massed gunfire was what was wanted. This in turn led to virtually all modern infantry tactics, from standardized unit organization to close order drill. And all this came about mainly because arrows were expensive to manufacture and archers difficult to train.[12]

With the gradual introduction of the musket and the rifle, the swing toward emphasis on quantity was in full force. It brought the revitalization of the infantry, the return to mass armies. Gunpowder, as Carlyle said, "makes all men alike tall."[13] More than the iron sword, more than the barbarian on horseback, more than the longbow, it proletarianized war. This process reached its culmination during the French Revolution in the *levée en masse* of 1793. After this, the "nation at arms" was a constant of European politics for 150 years, reaching its full flower in the two World Wars.

With the advent of nuclear power, the pendulum swung back sharply toward "quality." Notwithstanding the missile's enormous unit cost—$40 million per ATLAS or TITAN on a launcher plus $1 million per year per missile to keep them ready to fire—its tremendous destruction potential and, therefore, the relatively small numbers required well justified its development, production, and deployment.

Thus, the lesson of history is clear—neither cost nor effectiveness alone is a sufficient basis upon which to choose a weapon system. Both must be considered simultaneously and in relation to each other.

It should always be our policy to spend whatever is necessary for defense, but to spend whatever is spent in such a way as to achieve the greatest possible military capability—not to buy quality when the same amount spent on quantity will purchase greater effectiveness, and vice versa. Sometimes a weapon system with less than the maximum unit cost and effectiveness does win out as in the case of the new Navy attack aircraft, the A-7, which is far slower than many other aircraft now in the forces—and also much cheaper. The A-7 promises to be not only satisfactory for the missions it is intended to perform, but superior in those missions to alternatives which cost more per aircraft. As a Marine Colonel pointed out in an article last year—"Speed is not necessarily progress. . . . If . . . targets cannot be found and accurately hit, the effort is wasted."[14]

But sometimes it is just the other way around—cost-effectiveness studies lead us in the direction of higher quality, higher performance, higher unit cost. For example, during the past three years we have vastly increased the procurement of such relatively complex air-to-ground weapons as the radio-controlled BULLPUP close support missile, the SHRIKE antiradar missile, and other quality modern ordnance. They are far more expensive per unit than the older "free fall" bombs they displaced, but also far more effective. Our cost-effectiveness studies have shown that we get a more economical defense from these weapons than from bombs—even if the bombs are inherited and therefore almost cost free.

Cost-effectiveness studies or systems analyses are needed in the defense decision-making process for yet another purpose. This purpose might be labeled "how much is enough?" I noted earlier, in the previous lecture, that military requirements in the Department of Defense tend to be stated in absolute terms. The traditional military requirements study was typically a calculation of the forces required to achieve a single hypothesized objective.

To give an oversimplified example, suppose the objective were to achieve an expectation of destroying 97 per cent of 100 targets, using missiles having a 50 per cent single-shot "kill" capability. The tradi-tional requirements study would conclude that 500 missiles were needed because 100 missiles would achieve an expectancy of 50 kills, 200 missiles—75 kills, 300 missiles—87 kills, 400 missiles—94 kills, and 500 missiles—97 kills. This, of course, merely reflects the operation of the familiar law of diminishing returns. But the significant point is that the last 100 missiles would increase the "kill" expectation by only three extra targets, from 94 to 97. Thus, we should not only ask the question, "Do we need a capability to destroy 97 per cent of the 100 targets?"; we should also ask the question, "Is the capability to raise expected target destruction from 94 to 97 per cent worth the cost of 100 extra missiles?" In other words, we must not only examine total costs and total products but also marginal costs and marginal products.

Of course, when dealing with defense problems, data on marginal costs and marginal products do not, in themselves, imply mathematically what the number should be, i.e., the number we should buy. Since we do not operate in the market place, we cannot usually calculate the point where, in the business world, marginal cost equals marginal revenue. The defense decision-maker must exercise his own judgment as to whether the last 3 per cent of kill capability is worth the cost of another 100 missiles. But data of this kind can contribute a great deal to making that judgment an informed one.

The example I used is a relatively simple problem. At a much higher level of difficulty are such questions as whether an air defense system capable of destroying say 95 per cent of all the bombers an enemy could possibly launch against us is a desirable military objective. This depends not only on the cost of the air defense system itself but also on the relative costs and effectiveness of *other ways* of limiting damage to the United States, such as producing and deploying an antiballistic missile defense system, increasing our civil defense program, or adding to our strategic offensive forces. Thus, what are military objectives when viewed from one level, are simply means to a still higher objective when viewed from another level; and any given objective is likely to be only one of a number of alternative ways of achieving a still broader objective—in this case, limiting damage to the United States. The tradeoffs or substitution possibilities among them depend upon questions of cost and effectiveness, which in turn depend upon technology.

Although our national security objectives, in the highest sense of the word, reflect essentially the composite value judgments of the American people, the choice of a particular military strategy or military objective cannot be divorced from the cost of achieving it. Systems analysis at the national level, therefore, involves a continuous cycle of defining military objectives, designing alternative systems to achieve these objectives, evaluating these alternatives in terms of their effectiveness and cost, questioning the objectives and other assumptions underlying the analysis, opening new alternatives and establishing new military objectives, and so on indefinitely.

Thus, the problem of allocating resources within the Department of Defense itself involves the choosing of doctrines, weapons, equipment, and so forth, so as to get the most defense out of any given level of available resources or, what is logically equivalent, to achieve a given level of defense at the least cost. Approaching the problem from the first point of view—getting the most defense from a given level of resources— we work in terms of marginal rates of transformation and substitution. Approaching the problem from the second point of view—achieving a given level of defense at the least cost, which is the way Secretary Mc-Namara prefers to look at the problem—we work in terms of marginal products and marginal costs in order to help the top decision-maker choose the appropriate level of resources.

Regardless of which approach we use in allocating resources within the defense establishment, we must recognize that, at the highest level of government, there remains the problem of optimizing the allocation of resources across the entire spectrum of our national needs, and this means exercising choice among many desirable objectives. This in itself imposes certain constraints on the size of the defense budget at any particular time and under any particular set of circumstances. Certainly, if the international situation were to worsen, the value of an additional increment to the defense budget would be relatively greater than before, compared with other needs and concerns of the U.S. Government. Conversely, if the international situation were to improve markedly, then the value of the last increment of the defense budget would be relatively smaller than before, compared with our other needs. This problem of national choices is not unique to the United States. It is one with which the government of every nation has to cope, even, as we have seen, the Soviet Union.

But let me hasten to say that systems analysis or cost-effectiveness studies are by no means a panacea for all the problems of defense. Costs in general can be measured quantitatively, although not always with the degree of precision we would like. Measuring effectiveness or military worth poses a much more difficult problem. Reliable quantitative data are often not available. And even when such data are available, there is usually no common standard of measurement. This is particularly true with regard to systems analyses involving complex new technologies. Here, even reliable cost data are seldom available. Accordingly, the preferred alternative can rarely, if ever, be determined simply by applying a formula.

It has long been my contention:

that economic choice is *a way of looking at problems* and does not necessarily depend upon the use of any analytic aids or computational devices. Some analytic aids (mathematical models) and computing machinery are quite likely to be useful in analyzing complex military problems, but there are many military problems in which they have not proved particularly useful where, nevertheless, it is rewarding to array the alternatives and think through their implications in terms of objectives and costs. Where mathematical models and computations are useful, they are in no sense alternatives to or rivals of good intuitive judgment; they supplement and complement it. Judgment is always of critical importance in designing the analysis, choosing the alternatives to be compared, and selecting the criterion. Except where there is a completely satisfactory one-dimensional measurable objective (a rare circumstance), judgment must supplement the quantitative analysis before a choice can be recommended.[15]

I am the last to believe that an "optimal strategy" can be calculated on slide rules or even high-speed computers. Nothing could be further from the truth. Systems analysis is simply a method to get before the decision-maker the relevant data, organized in a way most useful to him. It is no substitute for sound and experienced military judgment, and it is but one of the many kinds of information needed by the decision-maker.

It is my experience that the hardest problems for the systems analyst are not those of analytic techniques. In fact, the techniques we use in the Office of the Secretary of Defense are usually rather simple and old-fashioned. What distinguishes the useful and productive analyst is his ability to formulate (or design) the problem; to choose appropriate objectives; to define the relevant, important environments or situations in which to test the alternatives; to judge the reliability of his cost and other data; and finally, and not least, his ingenuity in inventing new systems or alternatives to evaluate. My friend and former colleague, Albert Wohlstetter, used to insist that the systems analyst could contribute much more by inventing new systems than by comparing proposed systems; his own inventions are eloquent testimony to the validity of this view.

The analysis of rapid deployment of forces to trouble spots around the world illustrates many of these points. Early analyses (you may find one in *The Economics of Defense in the Nuclear Age*) concentrated on the question: what is the most economical type of aircraft to procure for the purpose? Sealift was regarded as much too slow to be a competitor. From an early date, extensive prepositioning of men and equipment, or of equipment only, was recognized as an alternative, or a partial alternative, and included in the analysis.

Then a systems analyst made an invention. A great problem with prepositioning is the difficulty of acquiring real estate for the purpose in foreign countries and the likelihood that the real estate, if acquired, and the prepositioned stocks will turn out to be in the wrong country (or even the wrong continent) when hostilities actually threaten or break out. So this analyst thought: why not pre-position on ships? A pregnant thought. We now have many "forward floating depots"—Victory ships stocked with Army equipment—in the Western Pacific, ready to steam to any threatened area and substantially augmenting our airlift rapid deployment capability.

At about the same time a more straightforward design development or "invention" produced the Roll-on/Roll-off, or "Ro-Ro," ship which can rapidly load and unload Army vehicular equipment at even primitive ports.

Then a third invention was made by an ingenious systems analyst who simply combined the characteristics of the forward floating depot and the Ro-Ro ship and developed an appropriate operational concept for the combination. This definitely made sealift competitive with air-lift for rapid deployment in many situations, and we have asked Con-gress in the 1966 budget for four specially designed Ro-Ro's to be used as forward floating depots.

Meanwhile some design inventions stimulated by airlift analyses promise us much more efficient airlift aircraft. The most important enables us to combine the marked economies of a very large aircraft with a landing gear and power plant which permit operations from short, primitive forward air bases. This combination promises to reduce or even eliminate the ground line of communication in the combat theater, with substantial savings in time, troops, and equipment. We are starting full-scale development of such an aircraft—the C-5A—this year.

Our analytic problem now is to determine the best mix of this better sealift and this better airlift. In many situations (e.g., close to the shore in SE Asia and Korea), the ships can win handily on cost-effectiveness criteria. In other hypothetical situations (e.g., farther inland), the C-5A wins handily. Each system has capabilities the other has not. And prob-lems the other has not. And different and difficult-to-analyze vulner-abilities to enemy action. No computer will automatically provide the answer to this problem of optimum mix, although a carefully formu-lated computer program can, under specified conditions, give valuable insights about break-even points and regions of sensitivity.

Typically in major systems comparisons this is the situation. There are multiple objectives or payoffs—not just one which is well defined and clear-cut. There are multiple circumstances in which the system may be called upon to function. And there are usually great uncertainties about costs, enemy intentions and capabilities, and other factors. This kind of systems analysis makes great demands on the analyst's ingenuity, his experience, and above all his judgment and common sense. When Ellis Johnson called it "quantified common sense," he was not far off the mark.

Finally, we must recognize that if the objectives or the costs or the measurements of military effectiveness are wrong, the answers will also be wrong. The SKYBOLT air-to-ground missile is a case in point. A gross underestimate of costs in 1961 led to a decision to carry that project into the production stage. When the full dimensions of the ultimate cost later became apparent, the decision was made to drop the project since it was not worth the increased cost in the light of the other alternatives available, namely, expanding the MINUTEMAN force and retaining more of the HOUND DOG air-to-ground missiles which were already in the inventory. You may recall that this decision led to some very painful moments with our British colleagues as the United Kingdom had also planned to use the SKYBOLT missile with its bombers. Our decision to drop the project created some very difficult problems for the British Government at the time and led to a meeting at Nassau between President Kennedy and Prime Minister MacMillan.[16] Yet, no responsible military or civilian official in our Defense Department or, I believe, in the British Defense Ministry, would argue in favor of the SKYBOLT today.

But notwithstanding all of these dangers I have mentioned, the need for systematic quantitative analysis in defense is much more important than in the private sector of the economy. Almost never do we find one person who has an intuitive grasp of all the fields of knowledge that are relevant to a major defense problem. We may be able to assemble a group of experts, each of whom has a good intuitive grasp of the factors relevant for answering one of the many subquestions and after discussion emerge with a fairly unequivocal answer. But in general, and especially when the choice is not between two but among many alternatives, systematic analysis is essential.

Moreover, in contrast to the private sector where competition provides an incentive for efficiency, efficiency in government depends on the conscious and deliberate selection of techniques and policies. And wherever the relevant factors are diverse and complex, as they usually are in defense problems, unaided intuition is incapable of weighing them and reaching a sound decision.

The need for systems analysis exists not only in the Office of the Secretary of Defense, that of the Joint Chiefs of Staff, and the headquarters of the military departments, but also at the other levels of the management structure in the defense establishment. After all, the purpose of this function is to help reduce the uncertainties involved in making choices among alternatives, and such choices have to be made at many different echelons. The areas of interest, the problems, and the subject matter will be different at these different levels, but the general approach—the way of looking at a problem—and the techniques will be basically the same.

Our objective, therefore, has been to build an integrated and mutually supporting structure of systems analysis throughout the defense establishment, with the broadest kind of exchange of information and techniques at and between various levels. This arrangement provides the checks and balances so essential to minimizing parochial viewpoints and organizational bias. The systems analyst, like any other scientist, must always be prepared to submit his work to critical scrutiny, and not just by other systems analysts. This is one of the great merits of the scientific method—it is an open, explicit, verifiable, and self-correcting process.

In addition to its "in house" capability, the Defense Department also supports a number of outside groups such as the Air Force's RAND Corporation, the Army's Research and Analysis Corporation, the Navy's Center for Naval Analyses, and the Defense Department's Institute for Defense Analysis. Whereas the "in house" systems analysis organizations can more easily achieve a close working relationship with the military experts, these outside supporting groups do have the advantage of greater detachment, of being better able to look at a problem with a fresh and relatively unbiased point of view. There is no question but that the systems analysis groups working within the defense establishment tend to take on the philosophical coloration of their sponsoring organizations, if for no other reason than that they are exposed to the same environment and same influences. Thus, there is a need both for an "in house" and an "outside" systems analysis capability.

In my own office I have a Deputy for Systems Analysis with a staff whose functions are to raise the quality of analysis throughout the Department, to see that studies requested by the Secretary are responsive to his needs, to review studies for the Secretary, and where necessary to do or re-do studies.

From a small beginning, systems analysis has now become a vital and integral part of the Defense Department decision-making process. The new programming function provides the link between planning and budgeting, relating both the forces and their resource costs to major military missions. Systems analysis provides the analytical foundation for the making of sound objective choices among the alternative means of carrying out these missions. Thus, the Secretary of Defense now has the tools he needs to take the initiative in the planning and direction of the entire defense effort on a truly unified basis.

IV | Retrospect and Prospect

IN THE COURSE of the three preceding lectures, I have sketched the evolution of the defense management problem over the years and discussed two of the major management innovations made since 1961. But although I have focused my attention on the central management system—the planning-programming-budgeting process—the Defense establishment is organized and managed in many different ways to perform its many different functions.

The principal operating subdivisions of the Defense Department are still the three military departments reporting directly to the Secretary of Defense. Most of the combat forces are organized in unified and specified commands, such as the Air Defense Command or the European Command, reporting to the Secretary of Defense through the Joint Chiefs of Staff. For certain services common to more than one of the military departments, there have been established over the years a number of what we now call "defense agencies" reporting to the Secretary of Defense either directly or through the Joint Chiefs of Staff. These include the Defense Atomic Support Agency, which conducts joint research and technical operations in the nuclear field; the Defense Communications Agency, which handles the over-all management of the long lines of communication; the Defense Intelligence Agency, which is responsible for military intelligence at the seat of the Government; the Defense Contract Audit Agency, which performs both precontract and postcontract audits; and the Defense Supply Agency, which provides logistics support involving common supplies and services for the entire defense establishment.

The last three organizations have been created since 1961, although the initial studies looking to the establishment of the Defense Intelligence Agency were completed under the previous Administration. The Defense Supply Agency was established in 1961 by putting together under one head a number of separate organizations handling particular categories of common supplies such as food, clothing and textiles, medical supplies, and so forth. This particular "defense agency," like the Defense Contract Audit Agency, reports directly to the Secretary of Defense rather than through the Joint Chiefs of Staff because of the essentially "nonmilitary" character of its activities.

The Secretary of Defense's own office is organized by fields of specialization—Research and Engineering, Installations and Logistics, Manpower, International Security Affairs, Comptroller, and so forth. His principal military advisors are the Joint Chiefs of Staff, and the principal military planners are in the Joint Staff organization of the JCS and in the military departments.

I pointed out in my second lecture that, even at the Secretary's level, we cannot manage all of the Department's activities solely in terms of programming. The pay, allowances, and other benefits of military personnel are prescribed by law, generally not with reference to particular assignments but, rather, in terms of an over-all career development pattern. Accordingly, we have to manage our military manpower in the aggregate, by grade, skill, etc., as well as in terms of program elements, such as B-52 wings or Army divisions.

There are many other areas, such as procurement policies and procedures, which cannot be effectively managed in terms of program elements. Still another management tool introduced in the last few years is the Department-wide Cost Reduction Program, a highly structured program with its own detailed goals, reporting channels, and postaudit system.

Finally, we must appreciate that the management tools needed by the Secretary of Defense may not necessarily suit the needs of management at the lower levels. For example, the financial data required by the commander of a military base to carry out his mission differ markedly from those required by the Secretary.

But all of these diverse organizations and functions must be harnessed together into a single effort directed toward a single overriding objective—the defense of the Nation, and this is the purpose of the planning-programming-budgeting system.

Looking back over the last four years, I believe it is fair to say that the planning-programming-budgeting system is now well established and is working smoothly. Admittedly, there are still difficult problems to be surmounted. One of these is the calendar. Although planning and programming have been designed as continuous activities, permitting changes to be proposed, considered, and decided at any time during the year, the third phase, budgeting, is still tied to the calendar. As large as it is, Defense's budget is only a part of the total United States Government budget which has long been presented to the Congress on an annual basis. And, indeed, the submission of the annual budget by the President is required by law.[1] There has been much talk over the years about two-year, three-year, or five-year budgets, but the Congress has made it plain, and for good and sufficient reasons, that it prefers to appropriate money annually, and I see no evidence that the Congress is about to change its mind on this point. But, as I indicated earlier, an annual budget, in itself, offers no particular obstacle—we simply take the first-year increment of the five-year program as the base for determining the financial requirements for that year.

The annual budget development cycle, however, does have an impact on the rest of the planning-programming-budgeting system. Because the President must submit the budget to the Congress in January, we require all components of the Defense Department to submit their budget requests to the Office of the Secretary of Defense early in October. This means that the comprehensive program review must be completed by middle or late August at the latest, and this, in turn, means that the proposed military plans and projected forces in the Joint Strategic Objectives Plan, prepared annually by the Joint Chiefs of Staff, and related requirement studies must be reviewed in the spring of the year. And thus, we find the entire planning-programming-budgeting system back on an annual cycle.

An annual cycle, in itself, should offer no particular problem if the entire review operation could be held to a strict schedule. Unfortunately, we have yet to achieve that ideal. As a result, the program and budget reviews have up until now tended to overlap in an undesirable way, making it difficult to reflect properly some of the force structure decisions in the support programs in time to assist in making budget decisions. But there is always another annual cycle, and we are hopeful that the schedule we have devised for this year's review will solve the problem, or come close to it. (I admit that we thought the same thing this time last year and were wrong.) There will always, inevitably, for good reasons as well as bad, be some program decisions that get postponed to the last possible moment—i.e., to the budget review.

In addition, we are making an effort to schedule the completion of the various detailed military requirement studies and other analytical efforts so as to maximize their value as information inputs into the force structure and program reviews. This is not easy. Scheduling the completion of cost-effectiveness studies is a little like scheduling the completion of Ph.D. theses. But to serve their purpose, these cost-effectiveness decisions must be an integral part of the entire planning-programming-budgeting process. Worthwhile analysis is not likely to be performed in a vacuum for very long. Where the information generated is not visibly used in the actual decision-making process, the capability to perform such analysis will wither. So the programming system has been designed to ensure through the program change procedures that the fruits of cost-effectiveness studies in the form of proposals for program changes will receive a timely and complete review.

The other less-than-satisfactory aspect of the programming system is our machinery for measuring and estimating costs. We have made improvements and progress during the past four years, but much more remains to be done.

There is first the problem of estimating the development and production costs of new weapon systems. The record of the Department over the past fifteen years in such estimating has been spectacularly bad. We and our contractors have typically underestimated costs by factors of two to ten. (Not 2 to 10 per cent, but 100 to 900 per cent.) An important cause has been our system of awarding contracts, in particular, the sequential awarding of development and procurement contracts, which places a premium on "optimistic" estimates by the contractor in the early bidding. We are trying, wherever feasible, to get away from the "cost plus" type of contract and the sequential letting of contracts. But we must also develop a much more adequate and sophisticated capability to make independent cost estimates—i.e., independent of contractor estimates.

We have had some promising successes in estimating aircraft and missile costs with multiple correlation techniques, developing estimating equations from past experience based on various physical and performance parameters. Errors of estimate are larger than we would like, but smaller than contractors' errors, and not biased as they are. To improve this technique we need many more trained people in the military departments and my office, and a large data bank, which does not now exist, of past cost experience reported on a uniform basis. We are introducing a new organization and reporting system known as the Cost and Economic Information System to provide the analysts and the data. It is just getting off the ground.

There is secondly the unsatisfactory state of operating costs in many areas. Our appropriation accounting systems do not directly yield operating costs by program element—e.g., by aircraft type. Many of the alleged "actual" operating costs of elements in the Five-Year Program are obtained by an arbitrary allocation of budget categories. Since these "actuals" constitute the base for projecting future operating costs, some parts of the financial program are not too meaningful. For example, we do not really know whether the Army's present cost projections accurately reflect the growing operation and maintenance requirements of its expanding fleet of aircraft. Improvements in the Department's cost estimating systems in the operation and maintenance area must definitely be placed high on our future agenda.

Because all major defense programs are now projected at least five years ahead, some early critics of the new system feared that it would tend to stifle change and place the defense effort in a straitjacket. I can assure you that their fears are unfounded. The Five-Year Program has proved to be quite amenable to change. Each year we consider three or four hundred program change proposals which, if they were all to be approved, would cause gross shifts in individual program amounts of $25 to $30 billion over the five-year planning period. Actually, the total gross value of changes, both plus and minus, which are approved each year, amount to somewhat less than half of this sum. I think we can safely conclude that constant change is likely to remain a characteristic of the Five-Year Force Structure and Financial Program.

However, the high volume and value of changes to the forward program do not lessen its worth to us as a management device. Indeed, one of the important purposes of any future plan is to indicate the areas where change may be desirable while there is still time to study, consider, and make such changes. In this respect, I think it is important to appreciate the role of the present leadership in instigating change. In developing the program, Secretary McNamara has chosen not simply to make decisions, but also deliberately to create opportunities to make decisions. He is constantly asking questions, requesting studies, goading the services and his staff to propose new alternatives, better alternatives to programs currently incorporated in the Five-Year Program. The criticism that the Secretary's management techniques stifle initiative and the development of ideas at the middle and lower levels of the Department seems to me to be the exact reverse of the truth.

Another criticism of both the programming system and the increased reliance on systematic quantitative analysis is that they have acted to "downgrade" the role of military judgment. I do not think they have. There is nothing inherent in the programming system or in systems analysis that calls for downgrading military judgment or for relying on computers for anything other than computation. In fact, I would say that the uniformed military planners have in recent years been given a greater opportunity to influence the Department's programs than they ever had previously. When planning and budgeting were separate, the planners, both in the JCS organization and the services, proceeded on their own, with little or no civilian control. But the plans they produced, because they were divorced from budget realities, were largely ignored in the actual decision-making process which determined the defense program. As I have mentioned before, prior to very recent years the Joint Strategic Objectives Plan was duly noted and filed, and the effective "real-world" decisions were made by the Secretary of Defense in the budget process, with no systematic participation by the military planners.[2]

This has completely changed. The Joint Chiefs of Staff, through the JSOP, now initiate the major proposals for changes in the approved Five-Year Force Structure. Moreover, their advice is solicited on every other program change proposal. In every way, the entire JCS organization is enmeshed in the planning-programming-budgeting system to a far greater extent than ever before. And with respect to the differences of opinion which inevitably arise, the truth is that on practically every serious issue affecting the defense program there are military and civilian partisans on both sides.

Criticism of the programming system is sometimes coupled with criticism of an alleged overcentralization of defense management generally. It is true, of course, that the institution of unified Defense Department-wide programming has provided the conceptual framework, the administrative mechanism, and much of the data needed to facilitate top-level decision-making. But these top-level decisions have always been made—if not explicitly, then implicly by the imposition of ceilings. As I noted earlier, priorities among major program objectives can be rationally determined only in the context of the total program, and balance among all elements of the defense effort can be achieved only at the Department of Defense level. The proper size of the MINUTEMAN force cannot be determined simply in terms of our ICBM requirements, or even in the context of the entire Air Force program. Being simply one element of the Strategic Retaliatory Forces, the MINUTEMAN program must be considered together with all of the other elements including the Navy's POLARIS force and, indeed, with all aspects of the general nuclear war problem. Similarly, the requirement for airlift aircraft operated by the Air Force could hardly be established independently of the requirement for sealift, and neither, independently of the requirement for lifting Army ground forces. This kind of centralized planning and decision-making is essential if soundly balanced military programs are to be pursued, and I think that few in the Department would now disagree.

In fact, the need was recognized with the creation of the National Military Establishment in 1947, when, for the first time since 1798, all of our armed forces were brought together again under one civilian head, and, for the first time, a consolidated budget was prepared for the entire Defense organization.[3] It was Secretary Forrestal's hope that the Joint Chiefs of Staff would produce a unified military plan which could serve as a basis for the annual budget, and it is interesting to note how he visualized the planning-budgeting process at that time:

First, the National Security Council must periodically evaluate the international situation . . . to assess and appraise the objectives, commitments, and risks of the United States in relation to our actual and potential military power. . . .

Second, the Joint Chiefs of Staff must, based on the evaluation . . . bring up to date the long-range strategic plans and prepare a correlated annual operating plan. . . . In the first instance this plan should be prepared on military considerations alone.[4]

He then described the role of the Research and Development Board and the Munitions Board and pointed out that on the basis of the over-all plans prepared by the Joint Chiefs of Staff and these two Boards, the military departments would develop their subsidiary plans. He then went on to say:

The next step is the preliminary pricing of these more detailed plans in order to get a picture of the cost . . . based on military considerations alone. If the aggregate of the price tags . . . is in excess of the amounts deemed by the President and his advisors to be allocable for defense purposes, the JCS must develop plans involving a lesser total strength, outlining the composition of such forces, a comparative necessity of programs, and the relative readiness to be achieved by each of the Services. This revised program must be developed within fiscal limitations.

*   *   *   *   *

The next step is the preparation by the JCS of a statement . . . which will clearly show the implications of lessened military effectiveness resulting from fiscal limitations. It is the duty of the Secretary of Defense, after assuring himself of their correctness, to make a presentation of the implications of lessened military effectiveness to the National Security Council in order that the risks may be evaluated and a decision reached as to the type and character of the military establishment which will best meet the international situation.

When the over-all plans have been adjusted to fit within the fiscal limitations, or after the further adjustment as a result of the National Security Council action, there must follow the preparation of final subsidiary plans within the Department.

The next step is the detailed pricing of these subsidiary plans. After internal scrutiny and review, the budgets will be ready for submission to the Secretary of Defense for final analysis and review . . .[5]

Thus, the major burden of preparing a "correlated" plan was to be placed on the Joint Chiefs of Staff. It never worked out that way. The JCS did eventually accomplish the first step, a plan prepared on the basis of military considerations alone (whatever that may mean), but they were never able to come up with a "revised program . . . developed within fiscal limitations." That task fell to the Secretary and his Comptroller, and that is how the dichotomy between military planning and budgeting, which I discussed earlier, developed.

The new National Military Establishment also created a need for an integrated, or at least a consolidated, defense budget, which, in turn, immediately raised the problem of uniformity in budget procedures and structures. The two entirely separate military departments, over the course of some 150 years, had each developed in its own way and each had its own pattern of organization, budgeting, and administration. Even within each of the departments there was no particular logic to the budget structure and system of accounts. Although the major appropriations, in general, paralleled the organization of each of the two military departments, they did not follow any particular functional pattern. Furthermore, there were a great many appropriation accounts for minor and often obscure purposes, the original justifications for which had long since been lost in 150 years of history.

The Navy Department, for example, as late as fiscal year 1948 was still managing its affairs through some 130-odd separate appropriation accounts, and the Congress for that fiscal year had actually appropriated new funds for eighty-seven of them.[6] These appropriation accounts ranged in size from fifty dollars for the payment of certain claims to $1,294 million for pay and subsistence of Navy personnel. There was even a separate appropriation of ten dollars for the U.S. Naval Academy Museum Fund in 1947. The situation in the War Department was no better.

When it is realized that each of these appropriation accounts has to be separately administered and accounted for, and that no funds may be transferred from one account to another unless specifically authorized by law, the problem which confronted the first Secretary of Defense is immediately apparent. It would have been virtually impossible for him to manage the defense establishment as a single enterprise, especially when another and different set of appropriation accounts was created for the new Department of the Air Force. Accordingly, Secretary Forrestal and his chief financial assistant, W. J. McNeil, decided to develop an entirely new, uniform budget structure for each of the three military departments. From their efforts there evolved the five major groupings of appropriation accounts which still exist today and which I have described in an earlier lecture.

The establishment of a uniform budget structure throughout the new military establishment was as revolutionary for its time as the establishment of the programming system was in 1961. As a matter of fact, it took about ten years to refine the system to its present form, and this was not accomplished without considerable agony throughout the Department. Indeed, it has been my observation that it is much easier to change policy than to change procedures. Perhaps the reason is that policy involves a relatively small group of people at the very top of the defense organization, whereas procedures involve literally tens of thousands, if not hundreds of thousands, throughout the entire establishment and the way in which they have been doing things day after day, year after year. So it is not surprising that the installation of the new programming system since 1961 has caused considerable anguish for much of the Defense Department.

Yet it seems to me that the programming function was the next logical step in the evolution of the defense management system. In fact, some efforts had already been made along programming lines on a unilateral service basis and without any official approval by the top management. The need was recognized and sooner or later some Secretary of Defense would have adopted some variation of it as a principal management tool. I feel confident that programming is here to stay. No doubt refinements and changes will be made; we have made quite a few ourselves over the last four years. But the basic scheme of things will survive until the next major advance in management techniques, whatever that may be.

However, there still exists, within the Pentagon, some scepticism as to the permanence of this particular management innovation, predicated on the proposition that "it takes a McNamara to make it work."

Often, of course, this is intended not as a serious indictment of programming, but simply as a kind of backhanded compliment to the talents of the Secretary. Yet some—remembering the relatively passive decision-making roles played by some other Defense Secretaries—are convinced that, under a significantly different style of leadership, the programming system and the data it generates would tend to go unused, and that the system itself would eventually atrophy and be discarded.

I will readily admit that to push through the development of the programming system in so short a time and make it work required a Secretary as strong and decisive as Robert S. McNamara. But I believe that the programming system can be adapted without too much difficulty to almost any style of leadership we are likely to have in the future. Every Secretary will have his own style—his own manner of approaching and making decisions—and management techniques must be adapted to the Secretary. I can easily imagine that some future Secretary, for example, will not want to get involved in as much program detail as Mr. McNamara. I see no particular problem in modifying the programming system to accommodate such a preference—without doing violence to any of the principal objectives of the system. We have "thresholds" in the system now, below which program changes can be made by the Secretaries of the military departments or at lower echelons.[7] There is nothing sacrosanct about the level at which such thresholds are established. But I cannot imagine a Defense Secretary who would willingly forego the assurance, provided by the new planning-programming-budgeting system, that his military plans are in proper balance and that the budgets he proposes are both fiscally responsible and actually provide the capabilities that his military planners are counting on. As President Truman pointed out at the end of World War II in his Message to the Congress proposing a single Department of Defense: ". . . strategy, program and budget are all aspects of the same basic decisions."[8] To this I would like to add, if I may be permitted to quote myself, that "the job of economizing, which some would delegate to budgeteers and comptrollers, cannot be distinguished from the whole task of making military decisions."[9]

But if programming, at least in its basic essentials, is here to stay, can the same be said for its partner in arms, systems analysis? I have pointed out that the programming system facilitates the use of systematic quantitative analyses comparing the costs and effectiveness of alternative programs. But programming is possible, indeed has been used, without systems analysis, and can achieve some of its important objectives—order, consistency, and rough intuitive balance among programs—without it.

I noted in the preceding lecture some of the objections raised against the use of systems analysis or cost-effectiveness studies in the solution of defense problems. Just the other day, I came across a new one in a study on "Science and Defense" prepared by Klaus Knorr and Oskar Morgenstern for the Center of International Studies of the Woodrow Wilson School of Public and International Affairs at Princeton.[10] The authors raised the question ". . . whether the recent emphasis on cost-effectiveness may not be too much of a good thing." They went on to say:

> Admittedly, sophisticated cost-effectiveness studies played too small a role until Mr. McNamara became Secretary of Defense. But there are fairly widespread feelings that its present role may be excessive and constitute an over-reaction to the previous lack.

The authors agree that cost-effectiveness studies are valuable in comparing similar weapon systems, but they question their utility in choosing between dissimilar weapon systems since they may "act as too sharp a brake on the innovating process that is concerned with radically new ideas."

Their main concern is with our ability to measure "effectiveness" in terms of numbers. This is a difficulty we have long recognized and one which I discussed at some length in my previous lecture. Indeed, in our book on *The Economics of Defense in the Nuclear Age,* we devoted a separate chapter to incommensurables and uncertainty.

But most surprisingly, the authors raised the question ". . . whether the POLARIS system would have been developed if cost-effectiveness notions had been applied then as they are today." They express ". . . grave doubts that the POLARIS system would have been developed or, if introduced, have been pushed as hard as has been the case. . . ." The fact of the matter is that almost no one was as enthusiastic about POLARIS as the systems analysts who were using *survivable* power as their measure of effectiveness. In 1961 almost the first thing Secretary McNamara did was to recommend to the President a doubling of the fiscal years 1961 and 1962 POLARIS programs from the then existing rate of five boats per year to ten per year. In addition, the entire program was accelerated so as to complete the tenth to the twenty-ninth POLARIS submarines in twenty months, viz., one per month, instead of the previous five per year schedule. At the same time we accelerated the development of the longer range POLARIS A-3 missile.[11] I recall that at the time this action was taken, we estimated that the average systems cost per POLARIS missile on or near station was probably two to three times that of a MINUTEMAN. An old-fashioned budgeteer using a simple *cost* criterion would indeed have looked askance at POLARIS. But its high survivability made it extremely attractive on a *cost-effectiveness* criterion. Thus, in this case, the application of the cost-effectiveness principle led to the program expansion of a relatively costly system.

With regard to the broader question concerning the proper role of cost-effectiveness studies or systems analysis in planning the research and development program, let me recall what I said about the organization of that program in my second lecture on programming. I pointed out that it was only in the third stage, "advanced development," that we "begin to explore the costs of the more likely applications in order to determine whether the potential operational benefit would be worth the cost of development, production, and deployment"—and even then the requirements test is a weak one. Projects proposed for the first two stages, "research" and "exploratory development," are not required to meet that test at all. And it is from these first two stages that the radically new ideas come.

It is worth noting that annual expenditures for research, exploratory development, and advanced development, which together constitute the area of new technology formation, have increased by 25 per cent since fiscal year 1962, to over $2.3 billion.

But although research and exploratory development, and even advanced development, do not necessarily have to be directly related to specific military requirements, full-scale engineering development or an operational system development—i.e., a decision to spend on the

order of $1 billion or more—can be justified only in terms of its po-
tential contribution to our strategy, considering both its costs and
military effectiveness, as well as the relative cost-effectiveness of other
alternatives. All too often in the past, systems development work was
started before consideration had been given to how the proposed
weapon system would be used, what it would cost, and whether its
contribution to our military capability would be worth its cost.

I would like to share with you a parable by Benjamin Franklin, for
which I am indebted to one of my predecessors as Defense Comptroller,
W. J. McNeil.[12] Franklin describes "How to make a STRIKING SUN-
DIAL, by which not only a Man's own Family, but all his Neighbors
for ten Miles round, may know what a Clock it is, when the Sun
shines, without seeing the Dial."

Chuse an open Place in your Yard or Garden, on which the Sun may shine
all Day without any Impediment from Trees or Buildings. On the Ground
mark out your Hour Lines, as for a horizontal Dial, according to Art, taking
Room enough for the Guns. On the Line for One o'Clock, place one Gun; on
the Two o'Clock Line two Guns, and so of the rest. The Guns must all be
charged with Powder, but Ball is unnecessary. Your Gnomon or Style must
have twelve burning Glasses annex't to it, and be so placed that the Sun shin-
ing through the Glasses, one after the other, shall cause the Focus or burning
Spot to fall on the Hour Line of One, for Example, at One a Clock, and there
kindle a Train of Gunpowder that shall fire one Gun. At Two a Clock, a Focus
shall fall on the Hour Line of Two, and kindle another Train that shall dis-
charge two Guns successively: and so of the rest.

Note, There must be 78 Guns in all. Thirty-two Pounders will be best for this
Use; but 18 Pounders may do, and will cost less, as well as use less Powder, for
nine Pounds of Powder will do for one Charge of each eighteen Pounder,
whereas the Thirty-two Pounders would require for each Gun 16 Pounds.

Note also, That the chief Expense will be the Powder, for the Cannon once
bought, will, with Care, last 100 Years.

Note moreover, that there will be a great Saving of Powder in Cloudy Days.

Kind Reader, Methinks I hear thee say, That is indeed a good Thing to
know how the Time passes, but this Kind of Dial, notwithstanding the mentioned Savings, would be very Expensive; and the Cost greater than the Advantage, Thou art wise, my Friend, to be so considerate beforehand; some Fools
would not have found out so much, till they had made the Dial and try'd it.
. . . Let all such learn that many a private and many a publick Project, are like
this Striking Dial, great Cost for little Profit.[13]

Now before we embark on a full weapon system development we conduct cost-effectiveness studies as well as technical studies. During this phase we, together with our contractors, do our thinking and planning. These studies not only permit us to define the program more clearly, assess better the technical risks, and determine the estimated costs and time schedule before we finally commit ourselves to a specific full-scale development, they also help us determine how well a proposed system might contribute to the attainment of our military objectives.

This is not to say that we can wait until the requirement for a new weapon system is already upon us before starting. The lead time from the initiation of engineering development to the operational deployment of a system is too long for that. In certain critical areas we must develop major weapon systems even though we are not sure that they will ever be deployed, or that a military requirement will actually emerge, and we do so wherever the risk is great enough to justify it. We buy an option.

The YF-12A Mach 3 interceptor is an example. The case for deployment of a force of such interceptors, at a cost of about $4 billion, would be much stronger if the Soviet Union were to deploy a force of new, supersonic, long-range bombers. Although they have not done so as yet, they may do so some time in the future, and we might not become aware of it until a prototype aircraft or even the first production aircraft was actually flying. To delay the start of development of a new interceptor until then might put us at a serious disadvantage.

Other similar programs exist. We spent about $1.5 billion in the development of the NIKE-ZEUS anti-ballistic missile system before we dropped it in favor of the development of a more advanced and effective system, the NIKE-X, for another $1.5 billion, even though the decision to produce and deploy the latter has still to be made. The new POSEIDON submarine-launched missile and our penetration aids program are in the same category. One of the major applications of the POSEIDON would be to give added insurance of being able to penetrate enemy anti-ballistic missile defenses. Our deterrent strategy depends upon our ability, under all foreseeable conditions, to destroy the attacker as a viable society, and this means that our strategic missiles must be capable of penetrating any kind of defense the Soviets may be able to devise. That is why we have spent almost $1 billion developing penetration aids during the period fiscal year 1962 through 1965. Though they may not represent a "new weapon system" to some, they give us an assurance that our missiles can penetrate defenses, which is worth far more than they cost.

I believe that much of the criticism directed against the technique of using cost-effectiveness studies or systems analysis is really related to specific decisions; people who for one reason or another dislike a particular decision attempt to fault the technique and rationale which led to it. Let it be said, here and now, that computers do not make decisions, and neither do systems analysts. The job of the systems analyst is to free the decision-maker from questions which can best be resolved through analysis, leaving to him those more difficult questions which can only be resolved on the basis of judgment. The systems analyst, for example, can tell the decision-maker how many more targets would be destroyed if 200 new bombers were added to the planned force and how much they would cost; he can rarely demonstrate whether they should or should not be added.

I would certainly agree that systems analysis is still in a very early stage of development, and much remains to be done in refining and making more efficient the tools of the trade—and even in devising better tools. But I am confident that it has passed the point in its development which medicine passed late in the nineteenth century where it begins to do more good than harm. It seems to me that anyone who has to make the kind of decisions which fall to the lot of the Secretary of Defense would want to have something more to rest on than unsubstantiated judgment, even though that judgment is based on extensive, if not wholly relevant, experience. Where a few numbers and a little calculation can help in making a good choice, I can see no reason why any Secretary of Defense would not want to use them. Accordingly, I feel certain that systems analysis, also, is here to stay— although the particular techniques employed will no doubt change over the years as will the way in which any particular Secretary chooses to use it. But the basic concept of economic choice, without which true "economy" can never be achieved, has now been firmly established in the Department of Defense. A recent Report of the House Armed Services Committee states the principle as well as anyone could:

No one would argue that nuclear propulsion is not better on a ship-for-ship basis, but in view of the increased cost the question really is which is the better—have fewer nuclear ships, each one somewhat superior, or more conventional ships of lesser capability for the same investment.[14]

There is a sort of inevitability about the trend toward unified Defense management ever since the end of World War II—here and in the military establishments of other major powers. It stems from the increasing complexity and unprecedented destructiveness of modern warfare and the need to achieve an optimum balance among all the elements of the military establishment. The Federal Republic of Germany rebuilt its military establishment after World War II within a strong, single Ministry of Defense. More recently, the British have reorganized their defense establishment within a single Defense Ministry and the Canadians are moving even more rapidly in the same direction.

On the other side of the Iron Curtain, all of the armed forces of the Soviet Union are under a Ministry of Defense. All components report to the Minister of Defense through the equivalent of a single Chief of Staff. Interestingly enough, one of these components is called the Strategic Rocket Troops. Unity of planning and operations appears to be a well-established concept in the Soviet Union. Marshal Sokolovsky, writing on "The Art of War in the Nuclear Age" last August, laid down the principle that:

... armed conflict ... will consist of coordinated operations by all of the branches of the armed forces, according to a single plan and under a single strategic leadership, aimed at fulfilling the immediate military-political and strategic tasks.[15]

In the Western World, some of our allies, notably the British, Canadians, and Germans, are also introducing programming and systems analysis into the management of their defense establishments. Although their problems are somewhat different from our own because of the nature of their national security objectives and the size and composition of their military forces, they believe that these techniques can contribute to the more effective management of their respective defense efforts.

The objectives, the organization, and the management techniques of national defense are all interrelated. Organization and procedures must be adapted to our changing national policies and objectives as well as to changes in the character of our resources and technologies. It will take all our ingenuity and skill to make these necessary adaptations so that we can continue to provide unified management of so great an enterprise as our present military establishment. At the beginning of our Constitutional history the building of three frigates and the management of a few companies to fight Indians were considered too great a task for the War Department alone.

Notes

CHAPTER I

[1] Gaither, A. Rowan, *Report of 10th Anniversary Session*, RAND Corporation, Board of Trustees, November 21, 1958. Unpublished.

[2] *A Century of Population Growth in the United States, 1790–1900*, Department of Commerce and Labor, Bureau of the Census, U.S. Government Printing Office, Washington, D.C., 1909.

[3] Bernado, C. Joseph and Bacon, Eugene, *American Military Policy*, The Military Publishing Company, Harrisburg, Pennsylvania, 1958, pp. 73 ff.

[4] Militia Act of May 8, 1792 (1 Stat 271).

[5] *Historical Statistics of the U.S.* Prepared by the Bureau of the Census with the cooperation of the Social Science Research Council, U.S. Government Printing Office, Washington, D.C., 1960, p. 737.

[6] Washington, George, "Fifth Annual Address to Congress, December 3, 1793." *Writings of Washington*, Vol. 33, U.S. Government Printing Office, Washington, D.C., 1940, pp. 163 f.

[7] Smelser, Marshall, *The Congress Founds the Navy*, University of Notre Dame Press, Notre Dame, Indiana, 1959, p. 73.

[8] A good account of the debate on the establishment of the Navy Department may be found in Smelser, op. cit.

[9] Paullin, Charles O., "Naval Administration Under the Navy Commissioners, 1815–1842," *Proceedings of U.S. Naval Institute*, Vol. 33, No. 2, Annapolis, p. 597.

[10] *Historical Statistics*, loc. cit.

[11] The size of the force reached 70,000 by 1901. See Ganoe, William A., *History of the U.S. Army*, Appleton-Century, New York, 1942, p. 413.

[12] *Regulations of the U.S. Army, 1895,* par. 187, U.S. Government Printing Office, Washington, D.C., 1901, p. 26.

[13] Nelson, Maj. Gen. Otto, "National Security and the General Staff," Infantry Journal Press, Washington, D.C., 1946, pp. 17 ff.

[14] Sherman, Gen. William T., *Memoirs,* C. Webster and Company, New York, 1892, Vol. II, p. 454.

[15] "Report of Secretary of War, December 1, 1902," *Annual Reports of the War Department for Fiscal Year Ending June 30, 1902,* U.S. Government Printing Office, Washington, D.C., 1902, Vol. I, p. 42 ff.

[16] The General Staff Act, February 14, 1903, P.L.–488, 57th Congress (32 Stat 830).

[17] Bernado and Bacon, op. cit., p. 301 ff.

[18] Paullin, Charles O., "A Half Century of Naval Administration in America, 1861–1911," *Proceedings of U.S. Naval Institute,* op. cit., Vol. 39, No. 3, p. 1259 ff.

[19] See Clark, W., *George Washington's Navy,* Louisiana State University Press, Baton Rouge, 1960.

[20] Washington, George, "Letter to Marquis de Lafayette, November 15, 1781," *Writings of Washington,* op. cit., Vol. 23, p. 341.

[21] Washington, George, "Letter to Count de Grasse, September 25, 1781," *Correspondence of General Washington and Count de Grasse,* ed. L'Institut Français de Washington, U.S. Government Printing Office, Washington, D.C., 1931, p. 48.

[22] For a detailed account of the correspondence between General Shafter and Admiral Sampson and its effect on the War, see Chadwick, French E., *Relations of U.S. and Spain, the Spanish-American War,* Scribner's Sons, New York, 1911, 2 volumes

[23] General Order No. 107, July 20, 1903; *General Orders and Circulars,* Headquarters of the Army, Adjutant General's Office, U.S. Government Printing Office, Washington, D.C., 1903.

[24] Legere, Maj. Lawrence, *Unification of the Armed Forces,* Unpublished Ph.D. Thesis, pp. 56–68.

[25] *Hearings on a United Air Service before the Subcommittee of the Committee on Military Affairs, House of Representatives, December 4, 1919,* U.S. Government Printing Office, Washington, D.C., 1919.

[26] Air Corps Act of 1926, P.L.–446, 79th Congress (44 Stat 780).

[27] The Joint Board, *Joint Action of the Army and the Navy,* U.S. Government Printing Office, Washington, D.C., 1935, Change 2, 1938, p. 5.

[28] "Special Message to the Congress Recommending the Establishment of a Department of National Defense, December 19, 1945," *Public Papers of the Presidents, Harry S. Truman, 1945,* U.S. Government Printing Office, Washington, D.C., 1961, p. 546.

[29] For reactions of official Army and Navy witnesses to various unification proposals, see *Hearings before the Committee on Military Affairs, U.S. Senate, 79th Congress, 1st Session, on S.84, 1945* and *Hearings before the Committee on Naval Affairs, U.S. Senate, 79th Congress, 2nd Session, on S.2044, 1946.*

[30] National Security Act, 1947, P.L.–253, 80th Congress, July 26, 1947 (61 Stat 495).

[31] *First Report of the Secretary of Defense, 1948,* U.S. Government Printing Office, Washington, D.C., 1948.

[32] National Security Act, Amendments of, 1949, P.L.–216, 81st Congress, August 10, 1949 (63 Stat 578).

[33] Reorganization Plan 6 of 1953 published in *U.S. Statutes at Large* (67 Stat 638).

[34] "Special Message to the Congress Transmitting Reorganization Plan 6 of 1953 Concerning the Department of Defense, April 30, 1953," *Public Papers of the Presidents, Dwight D. Eisenhower, 1953,* U.S. Government Printing Office, Washington, D.C., 1960, p. 61 ff.

[35] Reorganization Plan 1 of 1958; Department of Defense Reorganization Act of 1958, P.L.–599, 85th Congress, August 6, 1958 (72 Stat 514).

[36] "Special Message to the Congress on Reorganization of the Defense Establishment, April 3, 1958," *Public Papers of the Presidents, Dwight D. Eisenhower, 1958,* U.S. Government Printing Office, Washington, D.C., pp. 278 ff.

[37] "Report to Senator Kennedy from the Committee on the Defense Establishment," *New York Times,* December 6, 1960, p. 30.

CHAPTER II

[1] "Special Message to the Congress on Reorganization of the Defense Establishment, April 3, 1958," *Public Papers of the Presidents, Dwight D. Eisenhower, 1958,* op. cit., p. 278.

[2] For an interesting example of this technique see "Memorandum for the Secretary of the Army," June 6, 1960, signed by the Special Assistant to the Secretary of Defense, which outlines the budget guidelines set forth by President Eisenhower at a Cabinet meeting on June 3, 1960. Reprinted in the *Congressional Record,* June 30, 1960, p. 14027.

[3] *Hearings, Committee on Armed Services, United States Senate, 81st Congress, 1st Session, on S. 1269 and S. 1843, April 6, 1949,* U.S. Government Printing Office, Washington, D.C., 1949, p. 79.

[4] Letter from Representative George Mahon, Chairman of the House Subcommittee on Defense Appropriations to Secretary of Defense Neil McElroy, August 18, 1959 (unpublished).

[5] Letter from Representative George Mahon, Chairman of the House Subcommittee on Defense Appropriations to Secretary of Defense Thomas Gates, September 6, 1960 (unpublished).

[6] Hitch, Charles J. and McKean, Roland N., *The Economics of Defense in the Nuclear Age,* Harvard University Press, Cambridge, 1960, for the RAND Corporation, Santa Monica, California.

[7] Extract from the transcript of an interview with Secretary of Defense Robert S. McNamara on the National Broadcasting Company's program *Today,* February 17, 1961.

[8] "Statement of Gen. Maxwell D. Taylor," *Hearings, Subcommittee on National Policy Machinery, Committee on Government Operations, U.S. Senate, 86th Congress, 2nd Session, June 14, 1960,* U.S. Government Printing Office, Washington, D.C., 1960, p. 769.

[9] For example, see *House of Representatives Report No. 1607, 87th Congress, 2nd Session* (House Appropriations Committee Report on the Fiscal Year 1963 Department of Defense Budget, April 13, 1962), pp. 4 ff.

[10] For a further discussion of program element costs as well as a description of the Defense programming system in 1962 see: *Programming System for the Office of the Secretary of Defense, 25 June 1962,* U.S. Government Printing Office, Washington, D.C., 1963.

[11] For another, fuller description of the Defense programming system, see presentation and testimony of Assistant Secretary of Defense Charles J. Hitch, July 25, 1962. *Hearings, Subcommittee of the Committee on Government Operations, House of Representatives, 87th Congress, 2nd Session,* U.S. Government Printing Office, Washington, D.C., 1962, pp. 513 ff.

CHAPTER III

[1] From an editorial in the *Army–Navy–Air Force Register,* March 7, 1964.

[2] *Task Force Report on Budget and Accounting in the United States Government,* Commission on Organization of the Executive Branch of the Government, U.S. Government Printing Office, Washington, D.C., June 1955, pp. 11 ff.

[3] *Congressional Record,* Vol. 110, No. 77, April 21, 1964, p. 8287. Statement of Representative Melvin Laird.

[4] "Arms and the Atom—I," *New York Times,* May 14, 1957, p. 21.

[5] "Program of the Communist Party of the Soviet Union," *The Current Digest of the Soviet Press,* Vol. XIII, No. 46, p. 8.

[6] Khrushchev, N. S., "Speech to the Supreme Soviet, January 15, 1960," *The Current Digest of the Soviet Press,* Vol. XII, No. 2, p. 13.

[7] Alsop, Joseph, *From the Silent Earth,* Harper and Row, New York, 1954.

[8] *Ibid.,* p. 136.

[9] Fuller, Maj. Gen. J. F. C., *The Age of Valor,* Scribner's Sons, New York, 1945, pp. 25 ff.

[10] Kenworthy, Lt. Comdr. (R.N.) John M., *New Wars: New Weapons,* Elkin, Mathews and Marrot, London, 1930, p. 28.

[11] Fuller, op. cit., pp. 57 ff.

[12] Fubini, Eugene, "Down-to-Earth Research," *Ordnance,* March–April, 1964, Vol. 48, pp. 522 ff.

[13] Fuller, op. cit., p. 77.

[14] Reinburg, Colonel J. H., "Low Altitude, Close Air Support," *Army,* March 1964, pp. 29 ff.

[15] Hitch, Charles J. and McKean, Roland N., op. cit., p. 120.

[16] See text of joint communique and "Statement on nuclear defense systems" issued by President Kennedy and Prime Minister MacMillan, December 21, 1962 at Nassau, The Bahamas, *New York Times,* December 22, 1962, p. 3.

CHAPTER IV

[1] Budget and Accounting Act of 1921 (42 Stat 20).

[2] An interesting account of the budget-making process as seen by a former member of the Joint Chiefs of Staff can be found in General Maxwell D. Taylor's book, *The Uncertain Trumpet*, Harper and Brothers, New York, 1959.

[3] After remarks of Secretary of Defense James Forrestal on a radio interview, American Broadcasting Company Network, December 28, 1948.

[4] Statement of Secretary of Defense James Forrestal Before the Eberstadt Committee of the Hoover Commission, October 6, 1948 (unpublished). A close paraphrase of this quote can be found in the *First Report of the Secretary of Defense, 1948*, U.S. Government Printing Office, Washington, D.C., 1948, p. 41.

[5] *Ibid.*

[6] *The Budget of the United States Government for the Fiscal Year Ending June 30, 1948*, U.S. Government Printing Office, Washington, D.C., 1947, p. A87.

[7] For example, changes in the investment costs of a program element of less than $10 million in the first year and $25 million in total; or in the operating costs of a program element of less than $20 million in the first year and $50 million in total. (Department of Defense Directive 7045.1, October 30, 1964.)

[8] "Special Message to the Congress Recommending the Establishment of a Department of National Defense, December 19, 1945," *Public Papers of the Presidents of the United States, Harry S. Truman, 1945*, op. cit., p. 551.

[9] Hitch, Charles J. and McKean, Roland N., op. cit., p. 3.

[10] Knorr, Klaus and Morgenstern, Oskar, *Science and Defense: Some Critical Thoughts on Military Research and Development*, Policy Memorandum No. 32, Center of International Studies, Woodrow Wilson School of Public and International Affairs, Princeton University, February 18, 1965, p. 21 ff.

[11] "Special Message to the Congress on the Defense Budget, March 28, 1961," *Public Papers of the Presidents of the United States, John F. Kennedy, 1961*, U.S. Government Printing Office, Washington, D.C., 1961, p. 233.

[12] Used by the former Assistant Secretary of Defense (Comptroller) W. J. McNeil in a graduation address to the Industrial College of the Armed Forces, Washington, D.C., 1964.

[13] Franklin, Benjamin, *The Autobiography of Benjamin Franklin and Selections From His Other Writings*, ed. by Nathan G. Goodman, The Modern Library, New York, 1932, p. 201 ff.

[14] *Report of the House Armed Services Committee, House Document No. 271, 89th Congress, 1st Session*, April 29, 1965, p. 10.

[15] Sokolovsky, V. and Chedrednichenko, M., "The Art of War at the New Stage," *The Current Digest of the Soviet Press*, Vol. XVI, No. 38, p. 15.

2½m-9,'65 (F6453)